PREFACE

1. Scope

This publication provides joint doctrine for planning joint space operations.

2. Purpose

This publication has been prepared under the direction of the Chairman of the Joint Chiefs of Staff. It sets forth joint doctrine to govern the activities and performance of the Armed Forces of the United States in joint operations and provides the doctrinal basis for interagency coordination and for US military involvement in multinational operations. It provides military guidance for the exercise of authority by combatant commanders and other joint force commanders (JFCs) and prescribes joint doctrine for operations, education, and training. It provides military guidance for use by the Armed Forces in preparing their appropriate plans. It is not the intent of this publication to restrict the authority of the JFC from organizing the force and executing the mission in a manner the JFC deems most appropriate to ensure unity of effort in the accomplishment of the overall objective.

3. Application

a. Joint doctrine established in this publication applies to the joint staff, commanders of combatant commands, subunified commands, joint task forces, subordinate components of these commands, and the Services.

b. The guidance in this publication is authoritative; as such, this doctrine will be followed except when, in the judgment of the commander, exceptional circumstances dictate otherwise. If conflicts arise between the contents of this publication and the contents of Service publications, this publication will take precedence unless the Chairman of the Joint Chiefs of Staff, normally in coordination with the other members of the Joint Chiefs of Staff, has provided more current and specific guidance. Commanders of forces operating as part of a multinational (alliance or coalition) military command should follow multinational doctrine and procedures ratified by the United States. For doctrine and procedures not ratified by the United States, commanders should evaluate and follow the multinational command's doctrine and procedures, where applicable and consistent with US law, regulations, and doctrine.

For the Chairman of the Joint Chiefs of Staff:

CURTIS M. SCAPARROTTI
Lieutenant General, U.S. Army
Director, Joint Staff

Intentionally Blank

SUMMARY OF CHANGES
REVISION OF JOINT PUBLICATION 3-14
06 JANUARY 2009

- **Realigns space situational awareness as the fifth space mission area.**

- **Adds and defines protection and space deterrence within the space control mission area.**

- **Provides additional depth to the discussion of space debris and potential effects of collisions.**

- **Organizes space support mission area into assured access to space and satellite support operations.**

- **Highlights the links between defensive space control and space deterrence.**

- **Captures the role of non-Department of Defense (DOD) capabilities with regard to mitigation as well as options for the joint force commander.**

- **Refines the space coordinating authority.**

- **Describes the positive impact on deterrence that commercial and multinational space capabilities can provide by increasing resiliency of space architectures.**

- **Expands the list of entities with space operations roles and responsibilities.**

- **Updated to be consistent with national policy, DOD instructions, and other joint publications.**

Intentionally Blank

TABLE OF CONTENTS

Intentionally Blank

EXECUTIVE SUMMARY
COMMANDER'S OVERVIEW

- **Provides the Fundamentals of Military Space Operations**

- **Discusses the Space Mission Areas: Space Situational Awareness, Space Force Enhancement, Space Support, Space Control, and Space Force Application**

- **Explains the Command and Control of Space Forces**

- **Presents the Roles and Responsibilities for Space Operations**

- **Addresses Space Operations Planning and the Joint Space Tasking Order**

Fundamentals of Military Space Operations

Military Space Contributions to Joint Operations

Space capabilities have proven to be significant force multipliers when integrated into military operations. Space capabilities provide global communications; positioning, navigation, and timing (PNT); services; environmental monitoring; space-based intelligence, surveillance, and reconnaissance (ISR); and warning services to combatant commanders (CCDRs), Services, and agencies. To facilitate effective integration, joint force commanders (JFCs) and their staffs should have a common and clear understanding of how space forces contribute to joint operations and how military space operations should be integrated with other military operations to achieve US national security objectives.

Space and the Principles of Joint Operations

National security objectives and the needs of the supported commander compel the conduct of space operations. Space forces employ principles of joint operations and enable the application of the principles of joint operations by other joint forces.

Operational Considerations for Space

Space capabilities should be integrated and synchronized by the supported commander into specific joint offensive and defensive operations, operation and campaign planning, and into their concept of operations, operation plans (OPLANs), and operation orders. Space forces simultaneously support multiple users. This requires extensive coordination, planning, and the early identification of requirements and capabilities. Commander, United States Strategic Command

(CDRUSSTRATCOM), will prioritize space capabilities and make apportionment and allocation recommendations for Department of Defense (DOD) systems in coordination with supported commanders.

Characteristics of Space

The space environment has unique characteristics that impact military operations. Characteristics of space include:

No Geographical Boundaries. International law does not extend a nation's territorial sovereignty up to Earth orbit. Therefore, nations enjoy unimpeded satellite overflight of other nations through space.

Orbital Mechanics. Satellite orbits must follow certain orbital parameters due to laws of physics. Satellite operators can, in limited circumstances, change a satellite's orbital parameters, but this will deplete fuel, which can significantly degrade the performance or life-span of a system.

Environmental Considerations. The space environment is a significant limiting factor influencing every aspect of a satellite's size, weight, and power affecting the performance and life-span of any operational spacecraft.

Electromagnetic Spectrum (EMS) Dependency. Space-based assets depend on the EMS as their sole medium for transmitting and receiving information and/or signals. The electromagnetic frequency bands that space-based systems use are fixed and cannot be changed after launch. Therefore, it is vital that US forces achieve EMS control to ensure freedom of action for space assets.

Space Mission Areas

Space Situational Awareness

Space situational awareness (SSA) involves characterizing, as completely as necessary, the space capabilities operating within the terrestrial environment and the space domain. SSA is dependent on integrating space surveillance, collection, and processing; environmental monitoring, processing and analysis; status of US and cooperative satellite systems; collection of US and multinational space readiness; and analysis of the space domain. It also incorporates the use of intelligence sources to provide insight into adversary use of space capabilities and their threats to our space capabilities while in turn contributing to the JFC's ability to understand adversary intent.

Space Force Enhancement	Space force enhancement operations increase joint force effectiveness by increasing the combat potential of that force, enhancing operational awareness, and providing critical joint force support. Space force enhancement is composed of ISR; missile warning, environmental monitoring; satellite communications (SATCOM); and PNT.
Space Support	The space support mission area includes the essential capabilities, functions, activities, and tasks necessary to operate and sustain all elements of space forces throughout the range of military operations. Components of space support include: spacelift, satellite operations, and reconstitution of space forces.
Space Control	Space control supports freedom of action in space for friendly forces, and when necessary, defeats adversary efforts that interfere with or attack US or allied space systems and negates adversary space capabilities. It consists of offensive space control (OSC) and defensive space control (DSC). OSC are measures taken to prevent an adversary's hostile use of US/third-party space capabilities or offensive operations to negate an adversary's space capabilities used to interfere with or attack US/allied space systems. DSC are operations conducted to preserve the ability to exploit space capabilities via active and passive actions, while protecting friendly space capabilities from attack, interference, or unintentional hazards.
Space Force Application	Space force application is combat operations in, through, and from space to influence the course and outcome of conflict by holding terrestrial targets at risk. The space force application mission area includes ballistic missile defense and force projection capabilities such as intercontinental ballistic missiles.

Command and Control of Space Forces

Command Relationships	Joint space forces and capabilities are integral parts of military operations worldwide, requiring multiple command relationships between CDRUSSTRATCOM and the CCDRs. CDRUSSTRATCOM has the Unified Command Plan (UCP)-assigned role to conduct space operations. CDRUSSTRATCOM has designated the Commander, Joint Functional Component Command for Space (JFCC SPACE), to manage daily space operations. CDRUSSTRATCOM will determine command authorities

and delegate operational control or tactical control as appropriate. Normally, space forces supporting multiple geographic combatant commanders (GCCs) remain assigned or attached to United States Strategic Command (USSTRATCOM). However, there may be a need during operations for command of these resources to be transferred to a GCC.

Space Coordinating Authority

A supported JFC (when delegated space coordinating authority [SCA] from the GCC) integrates space capabilities and coordinates joint space operations in the operational area. Based on the complexity and scope of operations, the JFC can either remain SCA or designate a component commander (or other individual) as the SCA. The SCA has primary responsibility for joint space operations planning, to include ascertaining space requirements within the joint force.

Theater Space Network

Each GCC has space operators, resident on staffs at multiple echelons, who serve as theater advisors for national and foreign space capabilities (military, civil, and commercial). These individuals concentrate primarily on working the detailed activities of theater space operations in support of the SCA in developing, collecting, and prioritizing space requirements. Several DOD and national agencies deploy theater support teams that can provide additional space services and capabilities. Each Service uses different means to provide space expertise to satisfy the combatant command (CCMD) Service component's space support requirements.

Role of Non-Department of Defense Capabilities

CCDRs have requirements that cannot always be provided by DOD space capabilities alone. DOD space capabilities can be supplemented through national and foreign military, civil, and commercial capabilities.

Roles and Responsibilities

The Chairman of the Joint Chiefs of Staff

The Chairman of the Joint Chiefs of Staff will establish a uniform system for evaluating readiness of each CCMD and combat support agency (CSA) to employ space forces to carry out assigned missions and provide guidance to CCDRs for the employment of space capabilities and planning of joint space operations.

Geographic Combatant Commanders	GCCs will consider space capabilities when selecting alternatives to satisfy mission needs, as well as develop and articulate military requirements for space and space-related capabilities and provide prioritized theater space requirements to CDRUSSTRATCOM. They will integrate space services and capabilities into OPLANs, concept plans, campaign plans, theater guidance, and objectives, and plan for the employment of space capabilities within their area of responsibility.
Commander, United States Strategic Command	CDRUSSTRATCOM will plan and conduct space force enhancement, space support, DSC, SSA, and as directed, offensive cyberspace operations and space force application. CDRUSSTRATCOM will serve as the single point of contact for military space operational matters, except as otherwise noted. CDRUSSTRATCOM also has specific responsibilities related to strategic deterrence, cyberspace operations, electronic warfare, global strike, global missile defense, ISR, countering weapons of mass destruction, and analysis and targeting.
Joint Functional Component Command for Space	Commander, JFCC SPACE, coordinates, plans, integrates, synchronizes, executes, and assesses space operations as directed by CDRUSSTRATCOM. CDRUSSTRATCOM has delegated coordinating authority to Commander, JFCC SPACE, for planning of space operations in operational-level support of USSTRATCOM's UCP missions.
Other United States Strategic Command Functional Components	**Commander, United States Cyber Command,** as the supported commander for SATCOM, performs functions and activities of the SATCOM operational manager, including oversight, management, and control of SATCOM resources. **Joint Functional Component Command for Intelligence, Surveillance, and Reconnaissance** plans, coordinates, and integrates DOD ISR in support of strategic and global operations, as directed. **Joint Functional Component Command for Integrated Missile Defense** is responsible for operational planning in support of GCCs to include asset management of missile defense forces.
United States Strategic Command Service Component Space Operations	CDRUSSTRATCOM exercises command and control (C2) of assigned and attached space forces through JFCC SPACE, in coordination with Service component commands and their operations centers, including United States Army Space and Missile Defense Command/US Army Forces Strategic Command (USASMDC/ARSTRAT), Air Force Space Command (AFSPC)/14th Air

Force (AF) Air Forces Strategic (AFSTRAT), US Marine Corps (USMC) Forces USSTRATCOM (MARFORSTRAT), and US Fleet Forces Command.

Army Component

USASMDC/ARSTRAT conducts space and missile defense operations and provides planning, integration, control, and coordination of Army forces and capabilities in support of USSTRATCOM missions (strategic deterrence, global missile defense, and space operations); serves as the Army force modernization proponent for space, high altitude and ground-based midcourse missile defense; serves as the Army operational integrator for ground-based midcourse defense; and conducts mission-related research and development in support of Army Title 10, United States Code, responsibilities.

Marine Corps Component

MARFORSTRAT, as the USMC Service component to USSTRATCOM, represents USMC capabilities and space interests. Marine Corps requirements for space exploitation and space force enhancement are supported through MARFORSTRAT. MARFORSTRAT brings resident knowledge and access to Marine Corps capabilities that can support USSTRATCOM mission areas and advises CDRUSSTRATCOM on proper employment and support of USMC forces.

Navy Component

Commander, US Fleet Cyber Command (COMFLTCYBERCOM), Commander, Tenth Fleet (COMTENTHFLT), is the Navy's central operational authority for space in support of maritime forces afloat and ashore. COMFLTCYBERCOM COMTENTHFLT is responsible for directing operations of assigned space systems as an integral element of network operations and associated space control activities, and providing space expertise, support, products, and services, as required. US Tenth Fleet is the space support element for fleet satellite and ultrahigh frequency follow-on.

Air Force Component

AFSPC serves as the Air Force Service component to USSTRATCOM for space and cyberspace. In support of space operations, Commander, AFSPC, presents 14 AF, a component numbered air force (C-NAF), designated as AFSTRAT, to USSTRATCOM. The C-NAF commander then assumes tactical-level responsibilities of the Service component commander, as delegated by the AFSPC commander, to include operating space capabilities, and presentation, generation, readiness, and sustainment of Air

Force space forces assigned to CDRUSSTRATCOM. AFSPC operates the Air Force Satellite Control Network (AFSCN) which supports national security (defense and intelligence) satellites during launch and early orbit periods and is used to analyze anomalies affecting orbiting satellites. For particular constellations, the AFSCN provides routine control functions and operates a few satellite constellations with a dedicated control network.

Combat Support Agencies

The joint force uses DOD space capabilities supplemented by national and foreign civil and commercial partners. The CCDR's staff element is responsible for a specific function which works through its channels to the correct CSA (e.g., Defense Information Systems Agency [DISA], National Geospatial-Intelligence Agency, National Security Agency/Central Security Service, Defense Threat Reduction Agency, or Defense Intelligence Agency) to obtain the needed support or products. Information from other DOD agencies or United States Government organizations (e.g., National Reconnaissance Office, National Oceanic and Atmospheric Administration) is available through established procedures.

Commercial Space Operations

Commercial SATCOM are a critical part of US military operations, and planning should include protection of these services. DISA is the only authorized provider of commercial SATCOM for DOD.

Multinational Space Operations

Multinational space operations provide the joint force many opportunities, including increasing interoperability with and extending battlefield advantages to allies, demonstrating responsible behavior in space, and reassuring allies of our commitments to mutual defense. Partnerships can enhance collective security capabilities and can provide a deterrent effect against adversaries from attacking or interfering with friendly space capabilities.

Planning

Operations Plans and Space Operations

Commanders address space operations in all types of plans and orders, at all levels of war. Additionally, plans must address how to effectively integrate capabilities, counter an adversary's use of space, maximize use of limited space assets, and to consolidate operational requirements for space capabilities. Joint force planners incorporate space forces and capabilities into the basic plan and the applicable annexes. The completed plan should describe how space operations support the commander's stated objectives, how the adversary employs its space forces, the process and procedures through which additional support will be requested. **Annex N (Space Operations)** provides detailed information on space forces and their capabilities that the supported commander can use throughout the joint operation or campaign.

Operational Art and Operational Design

Since operational art integrates ends, ways, and means across the levels of war, operational art and operational design should be considered when planning space operations at all levels. A mix of DOD commercial, multinational, and allied space capabilities can support or enable operational art and operational design. They are a means to achieve the required end, or a way to support or enable other means to achieve the required end. As such, space forces and capabilities must be considered equally with forces and capabilities throughout the operational environment.

Key Planning Considerations

Space presents unique planning and operational considerations that affect friendly, adversary, and neutral space forces alike. Space capabilities require extensive and advanced planning. Space assets are sufficiently capable and robust; however, operational planners must understand the limited number of resources available and the distinct challenges with space force reconstitution. Numerous resource and legal considerations impact planning and affect mission success. The space planner understands planning and operational considerations for employment of space capabilities, and has a firm knowledge of the threats to the use of those systems by an adversary. The space planner must understand what can be done to limit an adversary's use of space capabilities and how to protect our own use of space.

Control and Coordinating Measures

Control and coordinating measures are used by JFCs to provide deconfliction between assets and missions, to maximize efficient and effective use of limited assets, and to provide effective C2 of forces and assets within a defined area. For most DOD space operations, control and coordinating measures are primarily accomplished through applicable guidance from CDRUSSTRATCOM and JFCC SPACE. CDRUSSTRATCOM operations orders provide and assure space capabilities by integrating subordinate component efforts to maintain strategic and operational advantages. The joint space tasking order development process does not account for missions performed by non-DOD space assets or those limited space forces assigned to a GCC, thereby creating potential conflicts between DOD and non-DOD agencies. It is then incumbent upon the GCCs and JFCC SPACE to coordinate as required to minimize conflicts.

CONCLUSION

This publication provides joint doctrine for planning joint space operations. It provides space doctrine fundamentals for all joint forces; describes the military operational principles associated with support from, through, and operating in space; explains Joint Staff, CCMD, USSTRATCOM, and USSTRATCOM functional and Service component relationships and responsibilities; and establishes a framework for the employment of space forces and space capabilities.

Intentionally Blank

CHAPTER I
FUNDAMENTALS OF MILITARY SPACE OPERATIONS

> *"Space power is a critical enabler to National Security and it is where the US has a competitive edge."*
>
> **General James E. Cartwright**
> **Vice Chairman, Joint Chiefs of Staff**
> **April 2011**

SECTION A. MILITARY SPACE CONTRIBUTIONS TO JOINT OPERATIONS

1. General

a. This publication provides guidance for planning, executing, and assessing joint space operations. It provides space doctrine fundamentals for all joint forces; describes the military operational principles associated with support from, through, and operating in space; explains Joint Staff, combatant command (CCMD), United States Strategic Command (USSTRATCOM), and USSTRATCOM functional and Service component relationships and responsibilities; and establishes a framework for the employment of space forces and space capabilities.

b. Space capabilities have proven to be **significant force multipliers** when integrated into military operations. Space capabilities provide global communications; positioning, navigation, and timing (PNT); services; environmental monitoring; space-based intelligence, surveillance, and reconnaissance (ISR); and warning services to combatant commanders (CCDRs), Services, and agencies. To facilitate effective integration, joint force commanders (JFCs) and their staffs should have a **common and clear understanding** of how space forces contribute to joint operations and how military space operations should be integrated with other military operations to achieve US national security objectives. To achieve optimal military utility from space, a basic understanding of space tools and the ability to coordinate activities between involved agencies and organizations and, when appropriate, integrate all necessary space capabilities with all other available capabilities (military, national, civil, commercial, and foreign) provides greater efficiencies and unified action. JFCs should establish a means to reasonably include appropriate outside agencies and organizations in operational planning, execution, and assessment activities.

c. US military use of space capabilities has changed significantly since military satellites were first placed in orbit. Continuous improvements in space technology have led to the development of more advanced space systems, as well as a host of commercially available capabilities. This has changed how commanders view space capabilities. Adversaries have also purchased and developed their own space capabilities. This has led to a situation where space is a congested, contested, and competitive environment.

(1) **Vulnerability**

(a) Military, civil, and commercial sectors of the US are **increasingly dependent** on space capabilities, and this dependence is a **potential vulnerability as space becomes increasingly congested, contested, and competitive.** Purposeful interference (PI) consists of deliberate actions taken to deny or disrupt a space system, service, or capability. PI with US space systems, including their supporting infrastructure, will be considered an infringement of US rights. Such interference, or interference with other space systems upon which the US relies, is irresponsible in peacetime and may be escalatory during a crisis. When practical and authorized, the joint force will protect civil, commercial, and foreign space capabilities.

(b) Commanders should consider the possibility of hostile actions from state and non-state actors intended to deny friendly forces access to, or use of, space capabilities while developing strategic estimates, plans, and other documents and planning future operations and activities. They also should anticipate the proliferation and increasing sophistication of space capabilities and products with military utility that could be used by any adversary for hostile purposes. Potential adversaries no longer have to develop large infrastructures to obtain or interfere with space capabilities. Today, many capabilities can be easily purchased. Options available to exert influence or prevent an adversary's access to space capabilities include diplomatic, informational, military, and economic measures.

(2) **Freedom of Action.** US forces should have the freedom to take advantage of the capabilities provided by space systems at a given time and place without prohibitive interference by the opposing force.

(3) **Protection.** Commanders should protect critical space systems and supporting infrastructure and take steps to assure availability of space-enabled mission-essential functions by developing techniques, measures, and relationships to maintain continuity of services.

(4) **Global Reach and Responsiveness.** Space-based capabilities are unique in that they are not subject to traditional air overflight restrictions and may already be in position to support operations when crises arise. However, there may be instances when the rapid surge of a capability, or the expeditious replacement of a capability, is required. In those cases, commanders should be aware that increasing capabilities of deployed space-based systems may be accomplished in hours to days, while development and deployment of replacement capabilities could take a year or more.

(5) **Space Deterrence.** Joint force operations contribute to the nation's multilayer approach toward deterring aggression against our space capabilities and infrastructure by:

(a) Promoting and demonstrating responsible behavior when employing space capabilities;

(b) Pursuing partnerships that encourage restraint in potential adversaries;

(c) Contributing to quick attribution for attacks;

(d) Protecting our space capabilities and infrastructures; and

(e) Implementing appropriate responses should deterrence fail.

d. Space systems provide specialized capabilities and offer global force enhancements critical to mission success. To realize the global advantage provided by space capabilities, JFCs must collaborate with USSTRATCOM and national agencies to ascertain military utility, vulnerabilities, and availability of space-enabled capabilities to achieve best efficiency and effectiveness.

2. Space and the Principles of Joint Operations

a. National security objectives and the needs of the supported commander compel the conduct of space operations. Space forces employ principles of joint operations and enable the application of the principles of joint operations by other joint forces.

b. Space capabilities enable the following applications of the **principles of joint operations:**

(1) **Objective.** The purpose of the objective is to direct military operations toward a clearly defined, decisive, and achievable goal.

(a) **Employing.** Commander, United States Strategic Command (CDRUSSTRATCOM), ensures that space objectives support and are aligned with the supported commander's objectives and are included in planning.

(b) **Enabling.** Space operations provide insight into the operational environment (OE) including adversary actions and capabilities. Space forces enable continuous dissemination of supported commanders' guidance.

(2) **Offensive.** The purpose of an offensive action is to seize, retain, and exploit the initiative.

(a) **Employing.** CDRUSSTRATCOM establishes and maintains freedom of action in space by ensuring the availability of space capabilities to the joint force while, when directed, denying the opposing force the same advantage.

(b) **Enabling.** Space forces provide globally available satellite communications (SATCOM); PNT; environmental monitoring; warning systems; and ISR capabilities and services. These capabilities support our leaders' efforts to employ the Armed Forces of the United States in coordination with the other instruments of national power to advance and defend US values and interests, achieve objectives consistent with national strategy, and conclude operations on terms favorable to the US.

(3) **Mass.** The purpose of mass is to concentrate the effects of combat power at the most advantageous place and time to produce decisive results.

(a) **Employing.** CDRUSSTRATCOM integrates and synchronizes supporting space forces to maximize effectiveness when concentrating combat power at the proper time and place. This integration and synchronization conserves available resources, minimizes impact on non-adversaries, and maximizes the effect on the adversary.

(b) **Enabling.** Space forces support the joint forces' ability to concentrate combat power at the proper time and place by providing SATCOM to coordinate and direct forces, ISR to facilitate situational understanding and targeting, and PNT to synchronize operations, navigate, and guide precision munitions.

(4) **Economy of Force.** The purpose of economy of force is to expend minimum essential combat power on secondary efforts in order to allocate the maximum possible combat power on primary efforts.

(a) **Employing.** CDRUSSTRATCOM implements apportionment and allocation prioritization guidance. Maintaining effective liaison with supported commanders enables CDRUSSTRATCOM to recommend appropriate space forces, actions, and levels of effort.

(b) **Enabling.** Space forces support JFCs in attaining information superiority, thereby reducing uncertainty and permitting reductions in the number and type of forces needed for secondary efforts. This allows commanders to concentrate forces and apply combat power at other points in the operational area. Space-based PNT enables joint force employment of precision munitions to minimize the number of weapons needed to create desired effects and minimize collateral damage.

(5) **Maneuver.** The purpose of maneuver is to place the enemy in a position of disadvantage through the flexible application of combat power.

(a) **Employing.** When necessary and feasible, CDRUSSTRATCOM directs the positioning of space forces to achieve advantage over adversaries. The employment of US space capabilities in multiple orbital regimes provides a standing position of advantage. This advantage includes freedom from overflight restrictions.

(b) **Enabling.** Space forces provide ISR, PNT, weather, and communications support to the joint force, enabling precise friendly force tracking (FFT), enhancing joint force situational awareness, maneuverability, and command and control (C2) effectiveness throughout the operational area. This enables the joint force to perform precise, coordinated maneuvers with speed, confidence, and stealth even in featureless terrain or under limited visibility.

(6) **Unity of Command.** The purpose of unity of command is to ensure unity of effort under one responsible commander for every objective.

(a) **Employing.** In order to execute the responsibility to advocate, plan, and conduct space operations for national security objectives, CDRUSSTRATCOM exercises combatant command (command authority) (COCOM) over assigned US military space forces. CDRUSSTRATCOM normally delegates operational control (OPCON) and/or tactical control (TACON) of assigned space forces to subordinate USSTRATCOM commanders. Unless otherwise directed by the Secretary of Defense (SecDef),

CDRUSSTRATCOM retains control of assigned space forces, even if they are deployed within the area of responsibility (AOR) of a geographic combatant commander (GCC). Space forces typically operate in general or direct support to other JFCs, with no reassignment of space forces or redelegation of operational authorities. This allows CDRUSSTRATCOM to maintain unity of effort, not only for space forces, but across all strategic forces CDRUSSTRATCOM must integrate and employ.

(b) **Enabling.** Supported commanders identify priorities to ensure supporting commanders and agency directors have clear guidance on the supported commander's intent, integrate space capabilities into planning and operations, and consider the impact if space capabilities are unavailable. Supporting commanders then provide details of how priorities are fulfilled. CDRUSSTRATCOM provides priorities and conflict resolution guidelines in support of joint space operations.

(7) **Security.** The purpose of security is to prevent the enemy from acquiring unexpected advantage.

(a) **Employing.** CDRUSSTRATCOM conducts continuous operations to establish and maintain space situational awareness (SSA), which includes assessment of the capabilities and intent of potential or actual adversaries. In turn, this supports development of defensive measures within fielded space capabilities, operational planning to defeat threats, and timely employment of available defensive measures to ensure the availability of operational space capabilities.

(b) **Enabling.** Space forces employ space-based ISR and missile warning capabilities with timely, assured, and responsive C2 systems. This enhances the joint force's ability to observe areas of interest (AOIs) and increases its situational awareness. JFCs maintain awareness of threats to space forces in their AORs and take measures to preempt or counter those threats in order to preserve US freedom of action in and access to space.

(8) **Surprise.** The purpose of surprise is to strike at a time or place or in a manner for which the enemy is unprepared. Surprise is closely linked to security, since security measures are often needed to achieve the element of surprise.

(a) **Employing.** CDRUSSTRATCOM's centralization of operational space C2 capabilities, coupled with effective SSA, contributes to comprehensive assessment and speed in decision making. This supports the ability of US forces to overwhelm adversaries' decision-making cycles, achieving surprise. Effective space control operations can negate threats and adversary efforts to interfere with or attack US or allied space systems.

(b) **Enabling.** Space operations provide timely information and data collection, enhanced information sharing, and precision targeting.

(9) **Simplicity.** The purpose of simplicity is to increase the probability that plans and operations will be executed as intended by preparing clear, uncomplicated plans and concise orders.

(a) **Employing.** CDRUSSTRATCOM provides authorities, intent, and guidance for space operations in orders and operational plans. This enables space forces to execute synchronized and mutually supporting operations with economy of force.

(b) **Enabling.** CDRUSSTRATCOM's guidance complements supported JFC plans and operations and provides a common understanding of required space capabilities.

(10) **Restraint.** The purpose of restraint is to limit collateral damage and prevent the unnecessary use of force. A single act could cause significant military and political consequences; therefore, the judicious use of force is necessary.

(a) **Employing.** In the conduct of space operations, CDRUSSTRATCOM observes the law of war, rules of engagement, and rules for the use of force.

(b) **Enabling.** Space forces contribute to the joint force's awareness of the OE and munitions accuracy.

(11) **Perseverance.** The purpose of perseverance is to ensure the commitment necessary to attain the national strategic end state.

(a) **Employing.** Satellites remain in their established orbits for years after deployment, and require long-term Service commitment to ensure continued availability.

(b) **Enabling.** Space forces enable persistent insight into adversaries' actions and disposition. This helps to dissuade potential adversaries from direct military confrontation, and fosters confidence in our situational awareness, thereby improving public resolve.

(12) **Legitimacy.** Gaining and maintaining legitimacy in the eyes of the local populace, host nation (HN) government, international audience, and US populace and Congress will assist the joint force in attaining the national strategic end state. Legitimacy is based on the legality, morality, and rightness of the actions undertaken.

(a) **Employing.** Adherence to law of war and compliance with US-ratified legal regimes enhances legitimacy in US military space operations. Most of the law relating to space activity is based on international treaties, rather than on customary law or teaching by scholars. The key treaty is the *Outer Space Treaty of 1967.* Legitimacy is further underscored by safe and responsible space operations.

(b) **Enabling.** Space forces help maintain high standards of accuracy in military operations (for example, precision guided munitions). Space forces also enable verification of other nations' compliance with treaty obligations and international mandates.

SECTION B. OPERATIONAL CONSIDERATIONS FOR SPACE

3. General

a. The importance of space operations is increasing due to the enabling capabilities they provide to the joint force. Space capabilities are vital to overall military mission accomplishment and provide advantages needed for success in all joint operations.

(1) Space capabilities should be integrated and synchronized by the supported commander into specific joint offensive and defensive operations, operation and campaign planning, and into their concept of operations (CONOPS), operation plans (OPLANs), and operation orders.

(2) Supported and supporting commanders coordinate, as appropriate, the deployment and employment of space forces required to accomplish the assigned mission.

(3) Space forces simultaneously support multiple users. This requires extensive coordination, planning, and the early identification of requirements and capabilities. CDRUSSTRATCOM will prioritize space capabilities and make apportionment and allocation recommendations for Department of Defense (DOD) systems in coordination with supported commanders. SecDef will determine solutions for the supported commander's needs that cannot be fulfilled by the supporting commander.

(4) The use of space capabilities by friend and foe alike is increasing in both volume and sophistication. Adversary knowledge of US space capabilities and the role of space assets in joint operations are considerable, and many resources are expended to constantly increase the awareness of technology and concepts of operation for current and planned space systems.

b. Commanders consider the following guidelines when planning and executing military operations, and when requesting space capabilities:

(1) Understand how others, including other United States Government (USG) departments and agencies, adversaries, partner nations, intergovernmental organizations (IGOs), and nongovernmental organizations (NGOs), use space capabilities to support military and civilian operations, and how the use of those space products/services may impact operational tempo and engagement outcomes (such as use of Global Positioning System [GPS] by civil aviation).

(2) Provide multinational partners appropriate access to systems and information. The joint force strives to provide necessary and appropriate space-related information at the lowest appropriate security classification level. However, established procedures for disclosure of intelligence information (specifically, information on US space systems and operations) must be followed in pursuing this goal. Furthermore, it is the responsibility of all original classification authorities to specifically consider releasability issues when creating documents and security classification guides.

(3) Look for opportunities in the evolving strategic environment to partner with other responsible nations, IGOs, NGOs, and commercial firms.

(4) Maintain an awareness of the space forces and their operational status.

(5) Understand how and why space capabilities are integrated across the range of military operations to include defense support of civil authorities (DSCA).

(6) Maintain SSA and assess the potential impacts on space-based and ground-based systems and operations.

(7) Evaluate the consequences of lost or degraded space capability and the availability of other means to perform the mission.

(8) Maintain and exercise military forces, plans, and capabilities for operating in and through a degraded, disrupted, or denied space environment.

4. Characteristics of Space

The space environment has unique characteristics that impact military operations. All commanders should have a basic awareness of the fundamental advantages and disadvantages offered by space operations in order to effectively employ space capabilities. Once considered a sanctuary, space is becoming increasingly congested, contested, and competitive. The number of objects in orbit around the Earth has grown dramatically over the years, increasing the potential for collisions. As more countries become space-faring nations and commercial and private interest continues to grow, competition for coveted orbits and radio frequency (RF) spectrum will continue to increase.

a. **No Geographical Boundaries.** International law does not extend a nation's territorial sovereignty up to Earth orbit. Therefore, nations enjoy unimpeded satellite overflight of other nations through space. Operating from space provides line of sight (LOS) access to large areas (including remote and denied access areas), which offers advantages for communications, navigation, ISR, indications and warning, and meteorological and oceanographic (METOC) information.

b. **Orbital Mechanics.** Satellite orbits must follow certain orbital parameters due to laws of physics. A satellite's orbit is chosen to best satisfy a satellite's mission. Satellite operators can, in limited circumstances, change a satellite's orbital parameters, but this will deplete fuel, which can significantly degrade the performance or life-span of a system.

c. **Environmental Considerations.** The space environment is a significant limiting factor influencing every aspect of a satellite's size, weight, and power affecting the performance and life-span of any operational spacecraft.

(1) **Space Weather.** Apart from the threat of meteorites, almost all hazards to space capabilities come from the sun. The various phenomena resulting from the sun's activity are collectively termed "space weather" and manifest as increased electromagnetic noise, ionospheric interference, or prolonged impact by energetic charged particles. Solar

flares, charged particles, cosmic rays, the Van Allen radiation belts, and other natural phenomena in space can affect communications, navigation accuracy, sensor performance, and even cause electronic failure.

(2) **Debris.** Operational satellites are under constant threat of impact. Orbiting particulates left behind during a satellite's lifetime, debris from satellite explosions or impacts, orbiting "trash" such as rocket bodies, or natural objects such as meteoroids, can damage operational systems. Further complicating this problem is that many of these pieces of debris are too small to track with current sensor capabilities. Currently, the US tracks only approximately 10 percent of space objects that are assessed by the National Aeronautics and Space Administration (NASA) to be a valid threat to spacecraft.

(a) **Debris Dispersal.** If an object detaches from an orbiting body, no matter what its size, it will initially follow the same orbit, varied only by the event that caused the breakup. This means that debris may take weeks, months, or even years to separate from its source; even clouds of objects, created by explosive events, will only slowly disperse once the initial explosion is complete. Depending on altitude and velocity, such objects may remain in a stable orbit for extended periods of tens or even hundreds of years.

(b) **Collisional Cascading.** The preferential use of certain orbits compounds the collision risk by concentrating large numbers of objects in discrete bands. There is growing awareness of the problem of congestion in space. While there are about 800 active satellites in Earth orbit, the United States Department of Defense Space Object Catalogue now provides details of nearly 21,000 space objects, each larger than around 10 centimeters. In addition, there are an estimated 300,000 items of untracked debris between one centimeter and 10 centimeters in size. As the orbital space around the Earth becomes increasingly cluttered, a future collision may create a runaway chain of events that creates collision after collision, rendering some orbits unusable for centuries. This is known as collisional cascading or the Kessler Syndrome.

d. **Electromagnetic Spectrum (EMS) Dependency.** Space-based assets depend on the EMS as their sole medium for transmitting and receiving information and/or signals. The electromagnetic frequency bands that space-based systems use are fixed and cannot be changed after launch. Therefore, it is vital that US forces achieve EMS control to ensure freedom of action for space assets.

See Appendix G, "Space Fundamentals," for additional information on space characteristics.

Intentionally Blank

CHAPTER II
SPACE MISSION AREAS

"Weather, intelligence, communications, precision [sic]-navigation-and timing...are all capabilities we have brought to the fight from the space domain and are relied upon in virtually any and every military operation."

Mr. Michael B. Donley
Secretary of the Air Force
November 2010

1. Introduction

US military space operations are composed of the following mission areas: space situational awareness, space force enhancement, space support, space control, and space force application. This chapter summarizes the role of each mission area and how they contribute to joint operations.

SECTION A. SPACE SITUATIONAL AWARENESS

2. General

SSA is fundamental to conducting space operations. It is the requisite current and predictive knowledge of the space environment and the OE upon which space operations depend. SSA involves characterizing, as completely as necessary, the space capabilities operating within the terrestrial environment and the space domain. SSA is dependent on integrating space surveillance, collection, and processing; environmental monitoring, processing and analysis; status of US and cooperative satellite systems; collection of US and multinational space readiness; and analysis of the space domain. It also incorporates the use of intelligence sources to provide insight into adversary use of space capabilities and their threats to our space capabilities while in turn contributing to the JFC's ability to understand adversary intent. SSA is a key component for space control because it is the enabler, or foundation, for accomplishing all other space control tasks.

3. Key Objectives

SSA supports the following key objectives:

a. Ensure space operations and spaceflight safety. SSA provides the infrastructure that ensures that US space operators understand the conditions that could adversely impact successful space operations and spaceflight safety (i.e., collision avoidance).

b. Implement international treaties and agreements. SSA is a means by which compliance, via attribution, can be verified and by which violations can be detected.

c. Protect space capabilities. The ability of the US to monitor all space activity enables protection of space capabilities, helps deter others from initiating attacks against space and terrestrial capabilities, and assures allies of continuing US support during times of peace, crisis, and conflict.

d. Protect military operations and national interests. SSA supports and enhances military operations.

4. Functional Capabilities

SSA can be divided into four functional capabilities (Figure II-1):

a. **Detect/Track/Identify (D/T/ID).** For SSA, D/T/ID is the ability to search, discover, track, maintain custody of space objects and events, distinguish objects from others, and recognize objects as belonging to certain types, missions, etc. D/T/ID's primary role is in support of safety of flight and support of offensive space control (OSC) and defensive space control (DSC) missions. This capability is required to provide the operations center data for creation of a common operational picture (COP) and presentation to the decision makers. The JFC benefits through comprehensive knowledge of inventory of space objects, events, and status, which may affect the user's missions.

b. **Threat Warning and Assessment (TW&A).** For SSA, TW&A is the ability to predict and differentiate between potential or actual attacks, space weather environment effects, and space system anomalies, as well as provide timely friendly force status. TW&A's primary role is in direct support of OSC and DSC and relies heavily on D/T/ID, characterization, and data integration and exploitation (DI&E). This capability is required to provide the JFC with an assessment of events related to space capabilities (all segments— space, link, and ground) and advanced warning of potential events of threats and their impacts to space capabilities or other capabilities dependent on space. These threat warnings and assessments may also contribute to or serve as indications and warnings of other potential events or threats, which might affect non-space capabilities and/or non-DOD capabilities and services.

c. **Characterization.** For SSA, characterization is the ability to determine strategy, tactics, intent, and activity, including characteristics and operating parameters of all space capabilities (ground, link, space) and threats posed by those capabilities. This provides the JFC, and other decision makers, with the knowledge and confidence to make assessments of space capabilities, objects, and events, which may affect the mission. Characterization of blue assets is necessary to support blue system anomaly resolution, establish baselines for evaluating adversary space object surveillance and identification capabilities and CONOPS and supports indications and warning development.

d. **Data Integration and Exploitation.** For SSA, DI&E is the ability to fuse, correlate and integrate multi-source data into a tailorable COP and enable decision making for the entire set of space operations missions. This capability enhances the other three functional capabilities of SSA and provides the ability to identify, correlate, and integrate multiple sources of data and information and to provide SSA services. These enhancements support

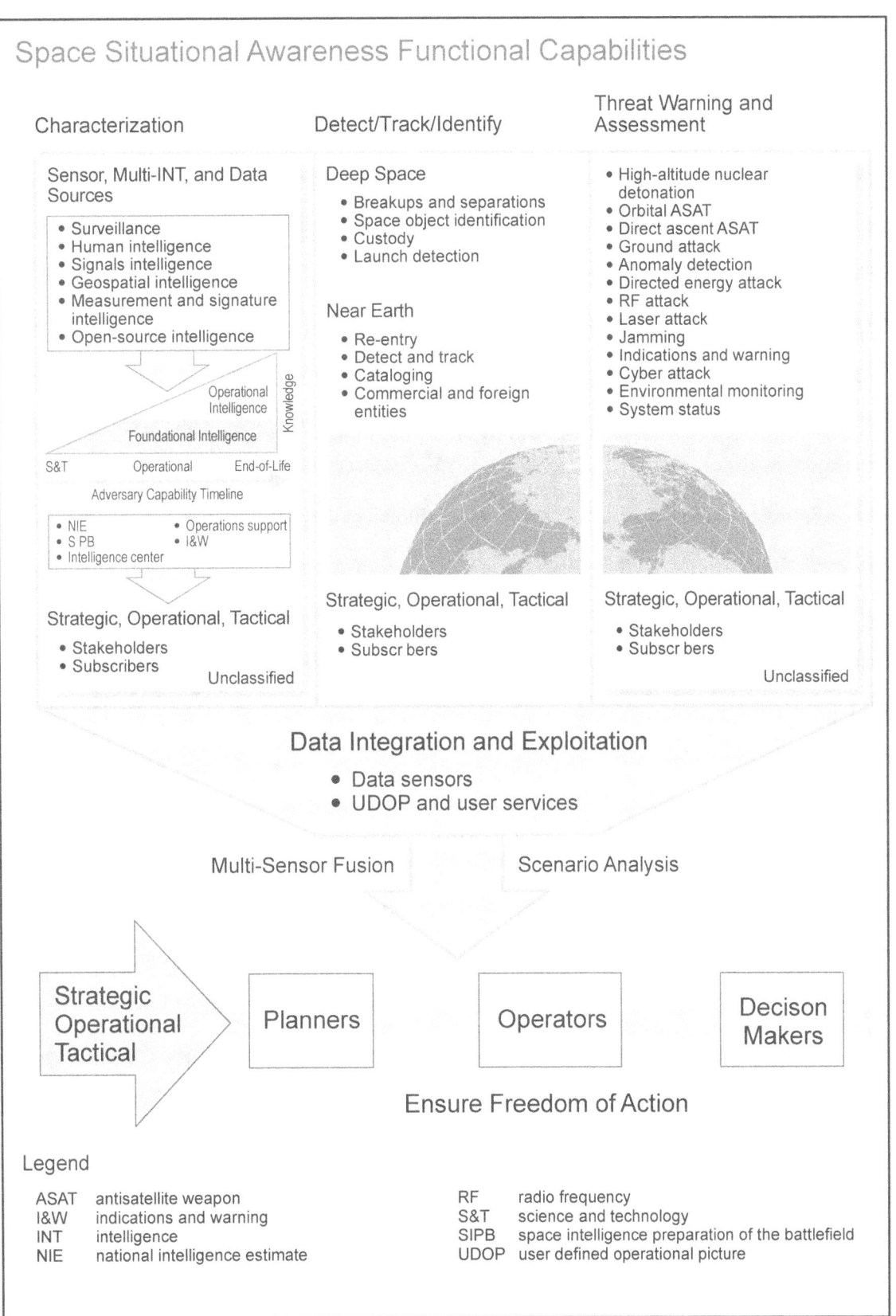

Figure II-1. Space Situational Awareness Functional Capabilities

the JFC and other decision makers by facilitating decision making (with earlier predictions at higher confidence) and more responsive courses of action (COAs) for space and non-space forces. DI&E should provide the information technology capability to:

(1) Search and discover better sources of data and information across multiple organizations, missions, and security levels;

(2) Rapidly integrate that data into real-time SSA operations centers;

(3) Identify to the operator or commander the discovery and context of changes as they occur;

(4) Retrieve, process, and store data according to its use (e.g., real-time or routine operations, training, rehearsal, research);

(5) Provide user-centric displays tailored to needs and access levels; and

(6) Provide these functions via operator-centric displays and tools that permit autonomous or manual execution as well as reminders and status of pending or ongoing tasks (e.g., blue force status).

5. Interagency Consideration

The overall SSA of the US can benefit from cooperation with non-USG satellite operators by gaining insight into commercial and foreign systems' status, mission capabilities, and maneuver plans. Potential satellite conflicts should be brought to the attention of USSTRATCOM. This cooperation also has the potential to reduce the demands on US space and intelligence systems. Multiple C2 nodes will often require SSA information, making unity of effort for SSA activities essential.

SECTION B. SPACE FORCE ENHANCEMENT

6. General

Space force enhancement operations **increase joint force effectiveness** by increasing the combat potential of that force, enhancing operational awareness, and providing critical joint force support. Space force enhancement is composed of ISR, missile warning, environmental monitoring, SATCOM, and PNT. They provide a critical advantage by reducing confusion inherent in combat situations. Space force enhancement operations also afford JFCs access to denied areas and persistence, which are not provided by comparable air, land, or maritime capabilities. Space force enhancement functions often are provided by other USG departments and agencies, commercial firms, consortiums, and multinational partners.

7. Components of Space Force Enhancement

a. **Intelligence, Surveillance, and Reconnaissance.** Monitoring AOIs from space helps provide information on adversary location, disposition, and intent; aids in tracking, targeting, and engaging the adversary; and provides a means to assess these actions through tactical battle damage assessment (BDA) and operational combat assessment. It also provides situational awareness, warning of attack, and feedback on how well US forces are affecting the adversary's understanding of the OE. In countering weapons of mass destruction (WMD), monitoring from space can characterize and locate adversary WMD capabilities and neutral, enemy, and friendly activities that may be sources of potential chemical, biological, radiological, and nuclear (CBRN) hazards. The support request procedures for products and information are dependent on the individual system. See Appendix A, "Space-Based Intelligence, Surveillance, and Reconnaissance," for more details.

b. **Missile Tracking.** Space-based systems, ground-based systems, correlation center C2 systems, and CCDR/national leadership decision support systems support time critical event conferencing. These systems provide allies and senior leaders the requisite timely warning and characterization of ballistic missile events to include launch, mid-course tracking, terminal phase re-entry, and nuclear detonations to support threat/non-threat determination and follow-on decision making.

c. **Launch Detection.** Space-based and ground-based sensors provide real-time and post-launch analysis to determine orbital characteristics and potential conjunctions with other objects in space. Detection of space launches is accomplished for both domestic and foreign launches. Launch detection data is used to evaluate events that could directly or indirectly threaten US or allied space assets. Similar to missile warning, this information is analyzed to determine potential impacts on assets so that timely warnings and recommendations for suitable countermeasures can be made. For domestic launches, this capability supports the characterization of nominal and anomalous space launch events.

d. **Environmental Monitoring.** Space forces provide data on meteorological, oceanographic, and space environmental factors that might affect military operations. Additionally, space capabilities provide data that forms the basis for forecasts, alerts, and warnings for the space environment that may negatively impact space assets, space operations, and their terrestrial users. Imagery capabilities can provide joint force planners with current information on sub-surface, surface, and air conditions (e.g., traffic capability, beach conditions, vegetation, and land use). Knowledge of these factors allows forces to avoid adverse environmental conditions while taking advantage of other conditions to enhance operations. Such monitoring also supports joint intelligence preparation of the operational environment (JIPOE) by providing the commander with information needed to identify and analyze potential adversary COAs. In support of military operations in CBRN environments, this monitoring also provides geospatial information (weather, terrain impacts on CBRN hazard transport/persistency) along with the assessment of a CBRN hazard incident on the natural environment.

e. **Satellite Communications.** SATCOM provides the JFC or subordinate commander with the ability to establish or augment telecommunications in regions of the world that lack suitable terrestrial infrastructure. The broad range of unique SATCOM capabilities allows the JFC to shape the OE. SATCOM uses include instant global connection to the Department of Defense information networks (DODIN), transmission of critical intelligence, the ability to tie sensors to shooters, and establish survivable communications in austere locations with limited or no infrastructure. The term SATCOM includes military, commercial, civil, and allied SATCOM systems. Allocation of SATCOM resources is governed by Chairman of the Joint Chiefs of Staff Instruction (CJCSI) 6250.01, *Satellite Communications*. For additional information, see Appendix D, "Satellite Communications."

f. **Positioning, Navigation, and Timing.** Space-based PNT assets provide essential, precise, and reliable information that permits joint forces to more effectively plan, train, coordinate, and execute operations. Assured PNT information is a mission essential element in virtually every modern weapon system. Precision timing provides the joint force the capability to synchronize operations and enables communications capabilities such as frequency hopping, as well as network and cryptological synchronization, to improve communications security (COMSEC) and effectiveness. PNT also enables precision attack from stand-off distances, thereby reducing collateral damage and allowing friendly forces to avoid threat areas.

g. **Navigation Warfare (NAVWAR).** NAVWAR refers to deliberate defensive and offensive action to assure friendly use and prevent adversary use of PNT information through coordinated space, cyberspace, and electronic warfare (EW) capabilities.

(1) Comprehensive NAVWAR effects are generated through coordinated, integrated, and synchronized space, cyberspace, and EW operations. NAVWAR is further enabled by supporting capabilities such as ISR and spectrum management.

(2) At the operational level, a JFC may gain a desired advantage by integrating diverse capabilities to create NAVWAR effects. Offensive and defensive NAVWAR operations must be integrated to ensure that friendly PNT information use is unimpeded when simultaneously attempting to deny adversary use of PNT information. When formulating NAVWAR COAs, JFCs should be cognizant of and balance intended NAVWAR effects and potential unintentional degradation to friendly forces' equipment and impacts to civil, commercial, and scientific users as stipulated by US national space-based PNT policy.

SECTION C. SPACE SUPPORT

8. General

The space support mission area includes the essential capabilities, functions, activities, and tasks necessary to operate and sustain all elements of space forces throughout the range of military operations.

9. Components of Space Support

a. **Spacelift.** Spacelift is the ability to deliver satellites, payloads, and material into space. Assured access to space includes spacelift operations and range operations.

(1) Spacelift operations are conducted to deploy, sustain, augment, or reconstitute satellite constellations supporting US military operations and/or national security objectives.

The use of commercial launch vehicles may be advantageous in certain instances to augment DOD launch capability. This aids the development of the US commercial space industry and supports the intent of the National Space Policy to leverage alternative space capabilities. Space launches are planned well in advance (often years) and executed in accordance with the established space launch manifest planners should account for the long lead times involved with the manifest scheduling process.

(2) Range operations are a key enabler of spacelift operations and include the capability to provide assured, responsive access to space safely and reliably. Space ranges provide operations support, launch traffic control, and scheduling services for spacelift operations. Launch ranges may also be responsible for planning and execution of spacecraft recovery operations.

b. **Satellite Operations.** Those operations conducted to maneuver, configure, operate, and sustain on-orbit assets.

(1) Satellite operations are characterized as spacecraft and payload operations. Spacecraft operations include telemetry, tracking, and commanding (TT&C), maneuvering, monitoring state-of-health, and maintenance sub-functions. TT&C is the process of monitoring spacecraft systems, transmitting the status of those systems to the control segment on the ground, and receiving and processing instructions from the control segment. Payload operations include monitoring and commanding of the satellite payload to collect data or provide capability in the OE. Satellite operations are executed through a host of satellite operations centers linked to on-orbit assets via dedicated and shared networks. Some systems utilize dedicated antennas for both mission data retrieval and routine satellite TT&C. Additionally, as a critical and essential link between the satellite operator and joint force, and a significant contributor to SSA, satellite operations include protection mechanisms to assure access to space assets.

(2) DOD satellites are monitored, sustained, and operated by Service component satellite operation centers. Globally dispersed antennas (e.g., those of the Air Force Satellite Control Network [AFSCN], the Naval Satellite Control Network, NASA networks, National Reconnaissance Office [NRO] and GPS ground antennas) provide the necessary links between the satellite operations centers and satellites to execute spacecraft and payload operations.

(3) Rendezvous and proximity operations (RPO) are specific processes where two resident space objects are intentionally brought operationally close together. Servicing of space assets requires the capability to rendezvous, conduct close proximity operations, and/or dock with the space asset. On-orbit servicing capabilities enable inspection, repair, replacement, and/or upgrade of spacecraft subsystem components and replenishment of spacecraft consumables (e.g., fuels, fluids, cryogens). RPO may also be used to provide information on spacecraft events. To minimize the risk of collision and the creation of orbital debris, all RPO activities should ensure space flight safety. RPO planners should coordinate with Joint Functional Component Command for Space (JFCC SPACE) to confirm space flight safety procedures are in place. For more information on RPO activities, planners should consult Department of Defense Instruction (DODI) 3100.12, *Space Support.*

c. **Reconstitution of Space Forces.** Reconstitution refers to plans and operations for replenishing lost or diminished space capabilities. This includes repositioning, reconfiguring unaffected and surviving assets, augmenting capabilities with civil and commercial capabilities, and replacing lost assets.

SECTION D. SPACE CONTROL

10. General

Space control supports freedom of action in space for friendly forces, and when necessary, defeats adversary efforts that interfere with or attack US or allied space systems and negates adversary space capabilities. It consists of OSC and DSC. These operations change in nature and intensity as the type of military operations change.

11. Components of Space Control

a. **Offensive Space Control.** OSC are measures taken to prevent an adversary's hostile use of US/third-party space capabilities or offensive operations to negate an adversary's space capabilities used to interfere with or attack US/allied space systems. OSC entails the negation of adversary space capabilities through deception, disruption, denial, degradation, or destruction actions. Adversaries, both state and non-state actors, will exploit increased access to space-based capabilities to support their operations. Therefore, the importance of space capabilities in military operations makes it incumbent on the US to prevent or negate adversary efforts that interfere with or attack US/allied space capabilities. OSC actions target an adversary's space-related capabilities and forces, using both lethal and nonlethal means. OSC operations support US national security actions taken to negate attacks against US and friendly space assets.

(1) **Prevention.** Prevention precludes an adversary's hostile use of US or third-party space systems/services to support their operations. Prevention can include diplomatic, informational, military, and economic measures, as appropriate. Prevention measures support space negation measures by allowing the US to use other instruments of national power. For example, diplomatic means could be used to persuade a commercial SATCOM provider to terminate commercial SATCOM services being used by an adversary. The US could also present evidence of an adversary's use of a third-party system and garner support for economic sanctions against the adversary. Prevention measures strengthen safety, stability, and security in space as well as maintain and enhance security advantages afforded to the US by space systems.

(2) **Space Negation.** Active defensive and offensive measures to **deceive, disrupt, degrade, deny,** or **destroy** an adversary's space capabilities. Measures include actions against ground, data link, user, and/or space segment(s) to negate adversary's space systems, or to thwart hostile interference with or attacks on US/allied space systems.

(a) **Deception.** Those measures designed to mislead an adversary by manipulation, distortion, or falsification of evidence to induce the adversary to react in a manner prejudicial to their interests.

(b) **Disruption.** Those measures designed to temporarily impair specific targeted nodes of an adversary system, usually without physical damage to the space system.

(c) **Degradation.** Those measures designed to permanently impair (either partially or totally) the utility of targeted adversary systems, usually with physical damage.

(d) **Denial.** Those measures designed to temporarily eliminate the utility of targeted adversary systems, usually without physical damage.

(e) **Destruction.** Those measures designed to permanently eliminate the utility of targeted adversary systems.

b. **Defensive Space Control.** DSC are operations conducted to preserve the ability to exploit space capabilities via active and passive actions, while protecting friendly space capabilities from attack, interference, or unintentional hazards. DSC can be a prelude to OSC operations.

(1) DSC includes operations that protect US or third-party space capabilities from adversaries' attack. For instance, by showing that an adversary is using a US or third-party system in a hostile manner, international pressure may be brought to bear against the adversary, thereby potentially forcing the adversary to cease its hostile actions. DSC actions protect friendly space capabilities from attack, interference, or unintentional hazards. Although focused on responding to man-made threats that can affect either terrestrial or space-based systems such as GPS and SATCOM jammers, DSC actions may also safeguard assets from unintentional hazards such as space debris, RF interference, and other naturally occurring phenomena such as radiation and weather.

(2) DSC preserves US access to, and use of, space by employing all means available to react to events affecting US and allied space capabilities. DSC is built on several elements including capabilities to detect and characterize an attack, ability to attribute an attack to an adversary, ability to defeat the attack, and the ability to operate through or deter an attack. A robust DSC capability influences adversaries' perceptions of US space capabilities and makes them less confident of success in interfering with those capabilities.

(3) DSC contributes to space deterrence by employing a variety of measures that help assure the use of space, and consistent with the inherent right of self-defense, deter others from interference and attack, defend our space systems and contribute to the defense of allied space systems, and if deterrence fails, defeat efforts to attack them.

SECTION E. SPACE FORCE APPLICATION

12. Space Force Application

Space force application is combat operations in, through, and from space to influence the course and outcome of conflict by holding terrestrial targets at risk. The space force application mission area includes ballistic missile defense and force projection capabilities such as intercontinental ballistic missiles. This mission area is incorporated into national space policy as well. Specific responsibilities can be found in DODI S-3100.13, *Space Force Application.*

CHAPTER III
COMMAND AND CONTROL OF SPACE FORCES

"Fully integrated {space} capabilities will provide depth, persistence, and reach capabilities for commanders at the strategic, operational, and tactical levels. Assured space systems and well-trained and experienced space professionals significantly reduce the fog, friction, and uncertainty of warfare."

Lieutenant General Richard P. Formica
Commander, United States Army Space and Missile Command/
Army Forces Strategic Command
11 May 2011

1. General

Specific command relationships are designated and discussed by the Global Force Management Implementation Guidance, and defined and described in Joint Publication (JP) 1, *Doctrine for the Armed Forces of the United States*. Applied to space forces, they establish and maintain unity of command, effort, and purpose in achieving joint force and national security objectives. CDRUSSTRATCOM advocates, plans, and executes military space operations and has the responsibility to prioritize, deconflict, integrate, and synchronize military space operations for current and planned joint operations.

2. Command Relationships

a. Joint space forces and capabilities are integral parts of military operations worldwide, requiring multiple command relationships between CDRUSSTRATCOM and the CCDRs. Therefore, clearly defined command relationships are crucial for ensuring timely and effective execution of space operations for the supported CCDRs. CDRUSSTRATCOM has the Unified Command Plan (UCP)-assigned role to conduct space operations. CDRUSSTRATCOM has designated the Commander, JFCC SPACE, to manage daily space operations. CDRUSSTRATCOM will determine command authorities and delegate OPCON or TACON as appropriate.

b. Normally, space forces supporting multiple GCCs remain assigned or attached to USSTRATCOM. However, there may be a need during operations for command of these resources to be transferred to a GCC. GCCs have the following responsibilities:

(1) Provide their prioritized space requirements to CDRUSSTRATCOM.

(2) Establish specific joint force guidance and objectives for space operations. This guidance is integrated into appropriate OPLANs and their annexes.

(3) Specify OSC and DSC objectives to be met, and provide guidance for the employment of C2 systems, communications systems, intelligence, logistics, and attack operations. This guidance should be reflected in appropriate OPLANs and their annexes.

The component commanders jointly conduct operations under the guidance and in support of the objectives of the GCCs.

(4) Consolidate, validate when necessary, and prioritize space operations requirements within their AORs from subordinate JFCs and component commanders for operations within their operational areas.

(5) May designate a space coordinating authority (SCA) and delegate appropriate authorities for planning, integrating, and coordinating space operations within the operational area.

3. Space Coordinating Authority

a. A supported JFC (when delegated SCA from the GCC) integrates space capabilities and coordinates joint space operations in the operational area. Based on the complexity and scope of operations, the JFC can either remain SCA or designate a component commander (or other individual) as the SCA. In selecting the appropriate option, the JFC considers the mission, nature, and duration of the operation; preponderance of space force capabilities made available; and resident C2 capabilities (including reachback). The SCA has primary responsibility for joint space operations planning, to include ascertaining space requirements within the joint force.

b. The SCA gathers operational requirements that may be satisfied by space capabilities and facilitates the use of established processes by joint force staffs to plan and conduct space operations. Following coordination, a prioritized list of recommended space requirements based on joint force objectives is provided to the JFC. Upon JFC approval, the list is submitted to the GCC for coordination with CDRUSSTRATCOM. To facilitate prompt and timely support, CDRUSSTRATCOM may approve direct liaison, as appropriate. This does not restrict CCMD Service component commands from communicating requirements directly to their counterpart USSTRATCOM Service component commander. However, SCAs keep their respective commanders apprised of all such coordination activities to ensure that space activities are coordinated, deconflicted, integrated, and synchronized. SCAs at subordinate commands, if designated, will accomplish the same requirements for submission to the CCMD SCA as directed. Summarizing, the SCA's roles and responsibilities include:

(1) Integrating space capabilities.

(2) Planning, coordinating, and synchronizing space operations in the operational area and ensuring inputs from the joint force staff and components are incorporated.

(3) Maintaining situational awareness of theater space operations, and coordinating with the CCMD SCA or Commander, JFCC SPACE, to integrate theater space operations into DOD space operations.

(4) Providing consolidated space requirements through the JFC for coordination as required.

JOINT SPACE ELEMENT

Recent joint operation experience has shown that the designated space coordinating authority (SCA) should consider establishing a joint space element to aid the SCA in the execution of day-to-day responsibilities. All Service components need to provide some level of support to the designated SCA to create synergy in space planning. The joint space element provides the Services and operational units in the operational area with a vehicle for planning space operations.

For example, in Operation IRAQI FREEDOM, the Commander, US Central Command (USCENTCOM) designated the joint forces air component commander as the SCA. The Army and Air Force provided support to the USCENTCOM SCA, creating a level of synergy in space planning. However, since there was no Navy representation on the SCA staff, the SCA provided direct space support to the lead carrier strike group (CSG) in theater. The CSG commander required direct liaison authorized in order to interact with the SCA at the operational level, for support to all tactical level maritime units.

Various Sources

4. Theater Space Network

a. Each GCC has space operators, resident on staffs at multiple echelons, who serve as theater advisors for national and foreign space capabilities (military, civil, and commercial). These individuals concentrate primarily on working the detailed activities of theater space operations in support of the SCA in developing, collecting, and prioritizing space requirements. If a GCC delegates SCA to a component commander, the GCC should maintain a space point of contact (POC) on the CCMD staff to coordinate space matters and maintain a link with the SCA. Several DOD and national agencies deploy theater support teams that can provide additional space services and capabilities.

b. Services assign space operators to various joint and Service echelons. JFCs may assign space experts to the joint force component commanders' staffs. JFCs and their components request space services and capabilities early in the planning process to ensure effective and efficient use of space assets. Each Service uses different means to provide space expertise to satisfy the CCMD Service component's space support requirements.

c. The Army integrates space capabilities at the army, corps, division, special forces groups, and fires brigade levels using space support elements (SSEs). SSE organic space experts are resident on the headquarters (HQ) staff as an integral part of the staff and are directly involved in the staff planning process from the beginning. The element is responsible for identifying opportunities to employ space force enhancement or space control, and then coordinating the required support. When deployed, the SSE establishes and maintains contact with the SCA. It also coordinates with the SCA on procedures for space support requests and reachback support. The SSE participates in the conduct of mission analysis to determine which space-based capabilities are applicable to the particular operation and then coordinates and makes recommendations for the allocation and use of space services and capabilities. The mission analysis performed by the SSE forms the basis of the staff's space running estimate, as well as annex N (Space Operations), for all orders and plans.

d. The Air Force integrates space capabilities through the director of space forces (DIRSPACEFOR). The DIRSPACEFOR is a senior Air Force officer with broad space expertise and theater familiarity. Air Force Space Command (AFSPC) ensures DIRSPACEFORs are qualified to perform their responsibilities, and the commander, Air Force forces (COMAFFOR), provides theater-specific information and orientation upon the DIRSPACEFOR's arrival. The DIRSPACEFOR facilitates coordinating, planning, executing, and assessing of Air Force space operations for the COMAFFOR, to include providing support for joint space operations to the SCA. The COMAFFOR can also direct the DIRSPACEFOR to support the SCA by providing advice on Air Force space forces. When the COMAFFOR serves as the joint force air component commander and is designated the SCA, the DIRSPACEFOR typically accomplishes the day-to-day duties assigned to the SCA.

e. At the operational level of war, Navy component commanders and numbered fleet commanders operate through their maritime operations centers (MOCs). MOCs support all assigned operational missions, C2 of assigned forces and employment recommendations to the respective JFC. Within the MOC, the space support working group (SSWG) provides support to all warfare areas, planning teams, and decision forums where space systems and services impact operations. The SSWG coordinates with the SCA as required, and ensures space-based capabilities and vulnerabilities are included in the deliberate planning process and that space requirements are integrated into each phase of the commander's operational plans. The SSWG also provides reachback support for assigned forces. The SSWG is tailored to meet individual MOC mission requirements and will most likely include reachback support from Commander, Tenth Fleet (COMTENTHFLT).

f. The Marine Corps conducts decentralized, combined arms operations and embraces the essential enabling capabilities of space-based systems on intelligence, cyberspace operations (CO), EW, and information operations (IO). Currently the Marine Corps does not operate any satellite systems, but functions as an equitable partner and active contributor to the National Security Space and joint space communities.

g. United States Cyber Command (USCYBERCOM) integrates cyberspace capabilities through the CCMDs' joint cyberspace centers. This includes integrating SATCOM with terrestrial communications for seamless management of cyberspace capabilities to support the joint force requirements.

5. Role of Non-Department of Defense Capabilities

a. CCDRs have requirements that cannot always be provided by DOD space capabilities alone. Accordingly, DOD's reliance on non-DOD space systems continues to grow. DOD space capabilities can be supplemented through national and foreign military, civil, and commercial capabilities.

b. Non-DOD capabilities can be leveraged to mitigate consequences of lost or degraded DOD space capability. This has a multi-layered effect by contributing to deterrence against further aggression or interference and by improving resilience of a particular capability, thereby improving mission assurance and the joint forces ability to operate in a degraded environment. Options include leveraging allied, foreign, and/or commercial space and non-space capabilities, as well as use of hosted payloads on a mix of USG, commercial, and allied platforms in different orbits, and employment of responsive space capabilities.

c. USSTRATCOM or other organizations will coordinate the appropriate assets to fulfill the required capabilities sought by the CCDR.

d. NASA has launch facilities and environmental Earth science products applicable to joint operations. The National Oceanic and Atmospheric Administration (NOAA), under the Department of Commerce (DOC), provides METOC information through the polar operational environment satellite (POES) system, geostationary OE satellites, DOD's Defense Meteorological Satellite Program (DMSP), foreign systems, and other environmental monitoring systems, as well as locating distress alerts via the search and rescue satellite-aided tracking (SARSAT) system. Additionally, commercial satellite programs such as Automatic Identification System and Long Range Identification and Tracking contribute to homeland security through global tracking of shipping traffic. The capabilities that many non-DOD agencies provide to joint forces are discussed in greater detail in Chapter IV, "Roles and Responsibilities."

Intentionally Blank

CHAPTER IV
ROLES AND RESPONSIBILITIES

"Operating within the increasingly congested, contested, and competitive space environment requires strategically reexamining our processes, planning flexibility, awareness of the space environment, and collaboration efforts with all spacefaring nations and corporations."

Lieutenant General Susan J. Helms
Commander, Joint Functional Component Command for Space
United States Strategic Command
11 May 2011

SECTION A. THE CHAIRMAN OF THE JOINT CHIEFS OF STAFF AND COMBATANT COMMANDERS

1. The Chairman of the Joint Chiefs of Staff

The Chairman of the Joint Chiefs of Staff (CJCS) will:

a. Establish a uniform system for evaluating readiness of each CCMD and combat support agency (CSA) to employ space forces to carry out assigned missions.

b. Develop joint doctrine for the operation and employment of space capabilities of the Armed Forces, and formulate policies for joint space training and military education of the Armed Forces.

c. Integrate space forces and their supporting industrial base into the Joint Strategic Capabilities Plan, and formulate policies for the integration of National Guard and Reserve forces into space activities.

d. Provide guidance to CCDRs for the employment of space capabilities and planning of joint space operations.

2. Geographic Combatant Commanders

GCCs also play a key role in space operations. Accordingly, they will:

a. Consider space capabilities when selecting alternatives to satisfy mission needs, as well as develop and articulate military requirements for space and space-related capabilities.

b. Provide prioritized theater space requirements to CDRUSSTRATCOM.

c. Integrate space services and capabilities into OPLANs, concept plans (CONPLANs), campaign plans, theater guidance, and objectives, and plan for the employment of space capabilities within their AOR.

d. Use staff elements and component commands to plan, monitor, advise, coordinate, and execute space operations within their AOR. If SCA is delegated to a component commander, the GCC should have sufficient space expertise on the CCMD staff to coordinate with the SCA and maintain situational awareness of space operations. If space operations support and coordination with the GCC's SCA is anticipated, GCCs should ensure that subordinate JFCs who are delegated SCA also have space POCs on their staffs.

e. Provide input to the Joint Staff for evaluations of the preparedness of their CCMD to carry out assigned missions by employing space capabilities.

f. Plan for and provide force protection for space infrastructure and forces assigned, deployed, and operating in their AOR.

SECTION B. UNITED STATES STRATEGIC COMMAND AND FUNCTIONAL COMPONENTS

3. General

a. With regard to the UCP-assigned space operations mission, the CDRUSSTRATCOM will:

(1) Plan and conduct space force enhancement, space support, DSC, SSA, and as directed, offensive cyberspace operations and space force application.

(2) Advocate for space capabilities.

(3) Provide military representation to USG departments and agencies, US commercial entities, and international agencies for matters related to military space operations, as directed.

(4) Serve as the DOD manager for human spaceflight operations.

(5) Provide warning and assessment of attack on space assets.

(6) Serve as the single POC for military space operational matters, except as otherwise noted.

(7) Plan, execute, and assess security cooperation activities that support space operations, in coordination with the GCCs.

(8) Conduct SSA operations for the USG, US commercial space capabilities, and services used for national and homeland security purposes; civil space capabilities and operations, particularly human space flight activities; and as appropriate, commercial and foreign space entities.

b. CDRUSSTRATCOM also has specific responsibilities related to strategic deterrence, CO, EW, global strike, global missile defense, ISR, countering WMD, and analysis and targeting. Accordingly, CDRUSSTRATCOM:

(1) Synchronizes plans for global missile defense, coordinates global missile defense operations support, and advocates for missile defense and missile warning capabilities.

For more information on missile warning and defense, see Appendix B, "Missile Warning," *and JP 3-01,* Countering Air and Missile Threats.

(2) Plans, integrates, and coordinates the security, operation, and defense of the DODIN, a responsibility that has been delegated to Commander, USCYBERCOM. Within the DODIN, space-based capabilities and services play a key role.

(3) In coordination with the CJCS, plans, directs, coordinates, and controls assigned space assets and forces for daily operations and crisis action planning in the event of military action against the US and/or its allies. In addition, USSTRATCOM provides warning to US national leaders of attacks against US space assets worldwide. USSTRATCOM executes these warning responsibilities through JFCC SPACE and its Joint Space Operations Center (JSPOC).

(4) Performs the functions, roles, and responsibilities of the strategic missile warning functional manager office (FMO) and the theater missile warning FMO that are collectively responsible for the management and oversight of the missile warning mission.

(5) Exercises COCOM over assigned space forces and assets.

(6) Ensures the availability of space capabilities to the joint warfighter.

(7) Implements apportionment and allocation prioritization guidance.

(8) Provides conflict resolution in support of joint space operations.

(9) Serves as the SATCOM Operational Manager for DOD. CDRUSSTRATCOM has operational authority for SATCOM on-orbit assets, control systems, and SATCOM terminal infrastructure. Directs day-to-day operation of DOD-owned SATCOM resources to provide authorized users with global SATCOM support as operations and evolving requirements dictate.

4. Joint Functional Component Command for Space

a. **Commander, Joint Functional Component Command for Space.** Commander, JFCC SPACE, coordinates, plans, integrates, synchronizes, executes, and assesses space operations as directed by CDRUSSTRATCOM. CDRUSSTRATCOM has delegated coordinating authority to Commander, JFCC SPACE, for planning of space operations in operational-level support of USSTRATCOM's UCP missions. The purpose of JFCC SPACE is to provide unity of command and unity of effort in the unimpeded delivery of joint space capabilities to supported commanders and, when directed, to deny the benefits of space to adversaries. JFCC SPACE responsibilities are reflected in the pertinent USSTRATCOM directives and/or orders. Commander, JFCC SPACE, exercises C2 of assigned space forces and ensures SSA through the JSPOC.

b. **Joint Space Operations Center.** JSPOC provides Commander, JFCC SPACE, with agile and responsive C2 capabilities to conduct space operations on a 24/7 basis. The JSPOC is built around an Air Force air and space operations center adapted specifically for space missions and global operations and provides reachback to CCDRs' SCAs. The JSPOC:

(1) Provides operational-level space C2 support to Commander, JFCC SPACE.

(2) Provides SSA and maintains the single integrated space picture that is shared with CCDRs and appropriate SSA users.

(3) Plans, directs, controls, integrates, and assesses space operations on behalf of CDRUSSTRATCOM and Commander, JFCC SPACE.

(4) Supports the intertheater responsibilities of Commander, JFCC SPACE, and coordinates with theater SCAs.

(5) Develops COAs, plans, and executes military space operations.

(6) Conducts day-to-day operations. When a space-related incident or contingency requires enhanced space support, the JSPOC assesses the situation and notifies the appropriate operations centers within USSTRATCOM and the National Military Command Center, as necessary.

5. Other United States Strategic Command Functional Components

a. **United States Cyber Command.** A subunified command, USCYBERCOM plans, coordinates, integrates, synchronizes, and conducts activities to direct the operations and defense of specified DODIN and is prepared to conduct military CO in order to enable actions throughout the OE. USCYBERCOM exercises OPCON or TACON of assigned and attached forces to secure, operate, and defend designated DODIN and conduct offensive CO when directed. Forces are employed for planning and executing global CO in accordance with assigned missions and orders. Commander, USCYBERCOM, as the supported commander for SATCOM:

(1) Directs the operation and defense of DODIN in support of DOD's full range of missions.

(2) Plans, coordinates, and oversees or directs SATCOM network plans.

(3) Performs functions and activities of the SATCOM operational manager, including oversight, management, and control of SATCOM resources.

(4) Coordinates with the Defense Information Systems Agency (DISA) to augment military satellite communications (MILSATCOM) with commercial SATCOM.

(5) Serves as a liaison among USSTRATCOM, DISA, and other users for SATCOM-related issues.

(6) Provides SATCOM status and resolution of outages or other problems from its Joint Operations Center using the Global Satellite Communications Support Center, satellite C2 centers, CCMD joint cyberspace centers, and other supporting elements, such as the regional satellite communications support centers (RSSCs).

For more information on CO, see JP 3-12, Cyberspace Operations, *and JP 6-0,* Joint Communications.

b. **Joint Functional Component Command for Intelligence, Surveillance, and Reconnaissance (JFCC ISR).** Plans, coordinates, and integrates DOD ISR in support of strategic and global operations, as directed. Develops allocation recommendations for ISR assets and associated processing, exploitation, and dissemination (PED) capabilities and high altitude deconfliction business rules in support of global force management of PED capabilities. JFCC ISR is also responsible for synchronizing global ISR with DOD collection requirements.

(1) The JFCC ISR AOI extends worldwide, from underwater to space and overlays, but does not affect AORs assigned to GCCs.

(2) JFCC ISR coordinates with multiple agencies which operate or use space capabilities, including the Defense Intelligence Agency (DIA), National Geospatial-Intelligence Agency (NGA), National Security Agency/Central Security Service (NSA/CSS), NRO, the Services, and other mission partners. Specific roles and responsibilities of JFCC ISR in relation to space operations are to:

(a) Develop and maintain a global COP of ISR which is shared in real time with JFCC SPACE, USSTRATCOM and other CCMDs, and JFCs via DODIN.

(b) Identify, define, and assess gaps, shortfalls, priorities, and redundancies of ISR capabilities.

(c) In support of CDRUSSTRATCOM's responsibilities as the ISR Joint Functional Manager, recommend allocation of airborne, space-based, and surface-based ISR resources to fulfill global and theater ISR requirements. JFCC ISR does this in coordination with JFCC SPACE and Joint Functional Component Command for Integrated Missile Defense (JFCC IMD) and appropriate CSAs on multi-mission sensors and requirements supporting space surveillance, missile defense and warning, and ISR operations.

(d) Coordinate with DIA (as the Defense Collection Manager) and JFCC SPACE in support of ISR-capable operationally responsive space (ORS) activities. Recommend allocation of ISR ORS capabilities.

c. **Joint Functional Component Command for Integrated Missile Defense.** The JFCC IMD is responsible for operational planning in support of GCCs to include asset management of missile defense forces. CDRUSSTRATCOM is the joint functional manager for missile defense and serves as the global synchronizer for missile defense planning. JFCC IMD coordinates with Services, CCDRs, and DOD agencies to identify and recommend through the joint force provider global DOD missile defense sourcing solutions.

For more information on missile defense, see JP 3-01, Countering Air and Missile Threats.

d. **Joint Functional Component Command for Global Strike (JFCC GS).** JFCC GS provides planning and force management in order to deter attacks against the US, its territories and bases, and when directed, defeat adversaries through decisive joint global strike.

SECTION C. UNITED STATES STRATEGIC COMMAND SERVICE COMPONENT SPACE OPERATIONS

6. General

CDRUSSTRATCOM exercises C2 of assigned and attached space forces through JFCC SPACE, in coordination with Service component commands and their operations centers, including United States Army Space and Missile Defense Command/US Army Forces Strategic Command (USASMDC/ARSTRAT), AFSPC/14th Air Force (AF) Air Forces Strategic (AFSTRAT), US Marine Corps (USMC) Forces USSTRATCOM (MARFORSTRAT), and US Fleet Forces Command. These Service components have distinct space missions. Common Service component responsibilities are to advocate for space requirements within their respective Services, provide a single POC for access to Service resources and capabilities, make recommendations to CDRUSSTRATCOM on appropriate employment of Service forces, provide assigned space forces to CDRUSSTRATCOM and CCDRs as directed, assist in planning support to space operations and assigned tasking, and support CDRUSSTRATCOM and other CCDRs with space mission area expertise and advocacy of desired capabilities as requested.

7. Army Component

a. USASMDC/ARSTRAT conducts space and missile defense operations and provides planning, integration, control, and coordination of Army forces and capabilities in support of USSTRATCOM missions (strategic deterrence, global missile defense, and space operations); serves as the Army force modernization proponent for space, high altitude and ground-based midcourse missile defense; serves as the Army operational integrator for ground-based midcourse defense; and conducts mission-related research and development in support of Army Title 10, United States Code (USC), responsibilities.

b. USASMDC/ARSTRAT contains two brigades. One provides space support, space force enhancement, and space control operations; the other provides space force application operations.

(1) USASMDC/ARSTRAT provides advanced geospatial intelligence (GEOINT), FFT, ballistic missile warning from deployed joint tactical ground stations, space expertise with Army space support teams, commercial satellite imagery products through commercial imagery teams, SATCOM planning by four RSSCs, and communication transmissions and satellite payload control of the wideband satellite constellation that includes Defense Satellite Communications System and Wideband Global Satellite Communications (WGS) and support to SSA.

(2) In its role of missile defense, USASMDC/ARSTRAT provides global missile defense forces to dissuade, deter, and defeat ballistic missile attacks.

(3) In its role for SATCOM, USASMDC/ARSTRAT is designated by CDRUSSTRATCOM as the wideband consolidated satellite communications system expert (C-SSE); military ultrahigh frequency (UHF) C-SSE for communication transmissions and for satellite operations management/payload control of wideband SATCOM and the military UHF SATCOM constellations. USASMDC/ARSTRAT is also the specific SSE for the WGS, the Global Broadcast Service (GBS), and the Mobile Users Object System (MUOS).

8. Marine Corps Component

a. MARFORSTRAT, as the USMC Service component to USSTRATCOM, represents USMC capabilities and space interests. Marine Corps requirements for space exploitation and space force enhancement are supported through MARFORSTRAT. MARFORSTRAT brings resident knowledge and access to Marine Corps capabilities that can support USSTRATCOM mission areas and advises CDRUSSTRATCOM on proper employment and support of USMC forces. During planning and execution, MARFORSTRAT informs the CDRUSSTRATCOM of changes in space capabilities that would significantly affect operational capabilities or mission sustainment. MARFORSTRAT assists in developing joint OPLANs and provides necessary force data to support all assigned missions to include deliberate or crisis action planning.

b. MARFORSTRAT directly supports subordinate functional components and Service component commanders on the proper employment of USMC forces and capabilities, assists in developing operational and exercise plans, and provides necessary force data to support all assigned missions, including the space mission through the Marine Corps space cadre. MARFORSTRAT provides support to facilitate planning, operations, and exercises for space through established policy and joint employment of assets to Marine Corps forces.

9. Navy Component

a. Commander, US Fleet Cyber Command (COMFLTCYBERCOM) COMTENTHFLT, is the Navy's central operational authority for space in support of maritime forces afloat and ashore. COMFLTCYBERCOM COMTENTHFLT is responsible for directing operations of assigned space systems as an integral element of network operations and associated space control activities, and providing space expertise, support, products, and services, as required. US Tenth Fleet is the SSE for fleet satellite (FLTSAT) and ultrahigh frequency follow-on (UFO).

b. COMFLTCYBERCOM COMTENTHFLT currently executes many of these duties through personnel assigned to Naval Network Warfare Command Space Operations directorate. COMFLTCYBERCOM COMTENTHFLT provides planners and space reachback for maritime forces and coordinates with other Service space operations entities, including space operations officers on strike group staffs, on joint force maritime component commander staffs, or maritime HQ.

c. Navy component responsibilities are to:

(1) Develop space effects packages (naval space plans for maritime forces) and provide space products in support of combat plans to satisfy strike group and forward deployed and theater maritime forces' requirements derived in the planning process.

(2) Provide SSA for maritime forces.

(3) Synchronize with the fleet staffs to provide operational assessment of maritime operations to facilitate translation of the maritime operator's space needs into actionable items and ensure delivery of critical space capabilities.

(4) Provide satellite vulnerability data products to maritime and other special customers.

d. The Naval Satellite Operations Center, assigned under COMFLTCYBERCOM, is responsible for operating, managing, and maintaining assigned narrow band satellite systems to provide reliable space-based services in direct support of Navy and joint forces. These systems include FLTSAT, UFO, MUOS, and varied payloads (Interim Polar and GBS).

10. Air Force Component

a. AFSPC serves as the Air Force Service component to USSTRATCOM for space and cyberspace. Its mission is to organize, train, and equip Air Force forces providing space control, force enhancement, space support and CO to the JFC. AFSPC accomplishes its mission through 14 AF, which oversees space launch and on-orbit checkout. These numbered Air Forces provide operational forces for space and cyberspace. Commander, AFSPC, provides strategic planning and develops CONOPS to support strategic-level operations. AFSPC is the specific SSE for advanced extremely high frequency (AEHF) and Milstar.

b. In support of space operations, Commander, AFSPC, presents 14 AF, a component numbered air force (C-NAF), designated as AFSTRAT, to USSTRATCOM. The C-NAF commander then assumes tactical-level responsibilities of the Service component commander, as delegated by the AFSPC commander, to include operating space capabilities, and presentation, generation, readiness, and sustainment of Air Force space forces assigned to CDRUSSTRATCOM. This C-NAF commander performs Service operational needs identification and prioritization, and supports Service-component aspects of deliberate and crisis action planning and integration for global and theater objectives.

c. The AFSPC commander is responsible for services, facilities, and range control for the conduct of DOD, NASA, and commercial launches from DOD ranges. Through control of DOD satellites, AFSPC provides continuous global coverage, operations for essential in-theater secure communications, environmental monitoring, and navigational data for joint operations and threat warning. AFSPC also operates ground-based radars to monitor ballistic missile launches around the world and guard against surprise attack. AFSPC assures access to space by providing launch and range operations for a variety of launch vehicles.

d. AFSPC operates the AFSCN which supports national security (defense and intelligence) satellites during launch and early orbit periods and is used to analyze anomalies affecting orbiting satellites. For particular constellations, the AFSCN provides routine control functions and operates a few satellite constellations with a dedicated control network.

SECTION D. SPACE-RELATED SUPPORT TO THE JOINT FORCE

11. Combat Support Agencies

The joint force uses DOD space capabilities supplemented by national and foreign civil and commercial partners. The CCDR's staff element is responsible for a specific function which works through its channels to the correct CSA (e.g., DISA, NGA, NSA/CSS, Defense Threat Reduction Agency [DTRA], or DIA) to obtain the needed support or products. Information from other DOD agencies or USG organizations (e.g., NRO, NOAA) is available through established procedures. The SCA can work with or through USSTRATCOM to establish additional support.

a. **Defense Information Systems Agency.** Provides services and support for a wide range of missions, including communications, C2, information assurance (IA), and DODIN services; and plays a key role in ensuring that US capability to operate in space is maintained. The Director, DISA:

(1) Acquires commercial communications services, including commercial satellite network assets for DOD.

(2) Defines system performance criteria for MILSATCOM systems, identifying areas of deficiency, and recommending corrective actions as appropriate.

(3) Assists USSTRATCOM with IA for SATCOM services.

(4) Provides MILSATCOM technical support, to include representation to international and North Atlantic Treaty Organization (NATO) forums.

(5) Provides teleport or gateway sites to support capacity in space.

For additional information, see Department of Defense Directive (DODD) 5105.19, Defense Information Systems Agency (DISA).

b. **National Geospatial-Intelligence Agency.** Supports US national security objectives by providing timely, relevant, and accurate GEOINT to the DOD, the intelligence community (IC), and other USG departments and agencies; conducting other intelligence-related activities essential for US national security; providing GEOINT for safety of navigation information; preparing and distributing maps, charts, books, and geodetic products; designing, developing, operating, and maintaining systems related to the processing and dissemination of GEOINT; and providing GEOINT in support of the combat objectives of the Armed Forces of the United States. NGA is a DOD agency and is designated a DOD CSA. NGA is also an element of the IC.

(1) NGA serves as the DOD lead for all acquisition or exchange of commercial and foreign government-owned imagery-related remote sensing data for DOD. NGA also serve

as the DOD lead for terrain environment modeling and simulation, coordinating with DOD modeling and simulation activities related to the geospatial aspects of natural and man-made features across the environmental domains of Earth, the atmosphere, and near-Earth space. As the DOD lead for GEOINT standards, NGA prescribes, mandates, and enforces standards and architectures related to GEOINT and GEOINT tasking, collection, processing, exploitation, and international geospatial information for the DOD components and for the non-DOD elements of the IC.

(2) NGA is also the functional manager for the National System for Geospatial Intelligence (NSG). NSG integrates technology, policies, and capabilities to conduct GEOINT in a multi-intelligence environment. NGA provides GEOINT to support senior national decision makers, and helps plan and prosecute military objectives. NGA's strategy supports operational readiness through a set of geospatial foundation data. This may include controlled imagery, digital elevation data, and selected feature information which can be rapidly augmented and fused with other spatially referenced information such as intelligence, weather, and logistics data. The result is an integrated, digital view of the mission area.

For additional information on GEOINT, see JP 2-03, Geospatial Intelligence Support to Joint Operations.

c. **National Security Agency/Central Security Service.** The NSA is the USG lead for cryptology, and its mission encompasses both signals intelligence (SIGINT) and IA activities. The CSS conducts SIGINT collection, processing, analysis, production, and dissemination, and other cryptologic operations. NSA/CSS provides SIGINT and IA guidance and assistance to the DOD components, as well as national customers. The Director, National Security Agency/Chief, Central Security Service (DIRNSA/CHCSS) serves as the principal SIGINT and IA advisor to SecDef, the Under Secretary of Defense for Intelligence, the DOD Chief Information Officer, the CJCS, the CCDRs, the Secretaries of the Military Departments, and the Director of National Intelligence (DNI), as well as other USG officials. NSA/CSS is designated a CSA of the DOD and is also an element of the IC. NSA/CSS's SIGINT mission helps protect the nation by providing information in the form of SIGINT products and services that enable national-level decision makers to make informed decisions and operate successfully. DIRNSA also provides IA advice and assistance regarding national security information and information systems to the USG departments and agencies, and serves as the National Manager for National Security Telecommunications and Information Systems Security. The joint force contacts the Overhead Collection Management Center for support.

d. **Defense Intelligence Agency.** Provides intelligence support to all CCMDs for a variety of missions, including, but not limited to, all-source military analysis, measurement and signature intelligence (MASINT), human intelligence, counterintelligence, cyberspace, IO, personnel recovery, peacekeeping and coalition support, indications and warning, targeting, BDA, collection management, and intelligence support to operations planning.

(1) DIA's core space-related functions include:

(a) Coordinating DOD and national technical collection policy with agencies having policy responsibilities for those systems.

(b) Facilitating and overseeing the PED of tailored and timely MASINT in order to help the joint force and national customers.

(c) Acting as the senior defense intelligence collection representatives and primary CCMD advocate for MASINT and technical collection capabilities.

(d) Characterizing the environment, threats, and challenges; and defining technical and operational capabilities in support of DOD and IC planning.

(e) Conducting evaluations and assessments on space-based collection capabilities supporting the DOD Intelligence Information System Enterprise.

(2) **Missile and Space Intelligence Center (MSIC).** MSIC is an element of DIA that produces finished, all-source scientific and technical intelligence in support of the CCMDs, force planners, and policymakers. It develops and disseminates scientific and technical intelligence on foreign threat systems, including guided missile systems, directed energy weapons, selected space programs or systems, and related command, control, and communications in support of operationally deployed forces and the materiel acquisition process. MSIC also develops and distributes digital simulations of threat weapon systems and provides threat simulation support to force developers and operational forces.

(3) **Defense Special Missile and Aerospace Center (DEFSMAC).** DEFSMAC is a collaborative DIA and NSA activity that provides tasking, technical support, analysis, and reporting for various DIA and NSA intelligence activities.

For additional information, see JP 2-01, Joint and National Intelligence Support to Military Operations, *and DODD 5105.21,* Defense Intelligence Agency.

e. **Defense Threat Reduction Agency.** DTRA is the DOD CSA responsible for countering WMD and addressing the entire spectrum of CBRN and high yield explosive threats. DTRA's programs serve to safeguard the US and our allies from the threat of WMD and include basic science research and development and operational support to US warfighters on the front line. The Director of DTRA is dual-hatted as the Director of the USSTRATCOM Center for Combating Weapons of Mass Destruction, which synchronizes countering WMD efforts across the CCMDs and leverages the people, programs, and interagency relationships of DTRA at the strategic level. This synchronization partnership is especially vital in developing and enhancing space capabilities for arms control and verification; CBRN defense and forensics; and WMD consequence management.

For additional information, see DODD 5105.62, Defense Threat Reduction Agency.

12. **Other Agencies and Organizations**

a. **National Reconnaissance Office.** A joint organization engaged in the research and development, acquisition, launch, and operation of overhead reconnaissance systems necessary to meet the needs of the IC and of DOD. NRO conducts other activities as directed by SecDef or the DNI.

(1) The Director, NRO, responsibilities include support to intelligence and warning, monitoring arms control agreements, and crisis support to the planning and conduct of military operations. The NRO liaison officers and theater support representatives located with each of the CCMDs serve as direct links to NRO for the CCDRs and their staffs.

(2) Taskings for NRO systems are accomplished through other agencies: GEOINT requirements are tasked through NGA, SIGINT requirements through NSA, and MASINT requirements through DIA. The basic reference for obtaining support is the *Joint Tactical Exploitation of National Systems Manual.*

For additional information, see JP 2-01, Joint and National Intelligence Support to Military Operations.

b. **National Air and Space Intelligence Center (NASIC).** NASIC is an Air Force organization that assesses foreign air and space threats. NASIC can provide deployed forces with unique aerospace intelligence capabilities for DOD operational commands, research and development centers, weapon acquisition agencies, and national planners and policymakers. In collaboration with other IC elements, NASIC's Counter Space Operations Cell provides foreign counterspace threat intelligence supporting military operations and serves as the primary NASIC focal point for operational defensive counterspace support. As such, NASIC is seen as the "all source intelligence integrator" for intelligence relating to suspected PI and electronic attack affecting DOD and USG space systems.

c. **National Ground Intelligence Center (NGIC).** The Director, NGIC, is responsible for ground-based counterspace-related, mobile EW systems; technical characteristics, performance, signatures, capabilities, limitations, and vulnerabilities of current and projected ground-mobile satellite jammers and EW systems impacting space capabilities.

d. **National Oceanic and Atmospheric Administration.** A component of DOC, NOAA provides many products with commercial, civil, and defense applications.

(1) NOAA has many programs and products with military applications, including:

(a) Operational Significant Event Imagery (OSEI)—broadcast, print, and Web-quality imagery created by the OSEI team of particularly significant or newsworthy environmental events which are visible in available satellite data. These events include dust storms, fires, floods, icebergs, ocean events, severe weather, hurricanes, and other events, each of which can impact military operations.

(b) National Geophysical Data Center—receives and archives Earth observations from space to include data from DMSP. The DMSP constellation, assigned to USSTRATCOM, is comprised of several near polar-orbiting satellites, monitoring the METOC and solar-terrestrial environments.

(2) NOAA operates the Space Weather Prediction Center (SWPC) as part of the National Weather Service. SWPC supports the USG and civilian space weather customer base. In addition, SWPC partners with the Air Force Weather Agency (AFWA) space weather production center to provide support to DOD. The two organizations work together to provide real-time monitoring and forecasting of solar and near-Earth space weather events that impact military operations. AFWA leverages SWPC's research and technique development capabilities to improve space weather support to military operations.

(3) NOAA's operational environmental satellite system is composed of geostationary and polar orbiting satellites. Both kinds of satellites are necessary for providing a complete global weather monitoring system. The satellites also carry additional instruments which are used to support aviation safety and maritime/shipping safety which can impact military operations.

(4) NOAA also operates SARSAT which is a global search and rescue (SAR) system that detects and locates distress signals from emergency beacons carried by mariners, aviators, and land-based users and then relays this information to SAR authorities around the world. SARSAT's global-reach is designed to primarily support civilian users; however, the system also supports military units particularly in permissive OEs. DOD use of the SARSAT system is promulgated by DODI 3003.01, *DOD Support to Civil Search and Rescue (SAR)*.

e. **Missile Defense Agency (MDA).** The MDA's mission is to develop, test, and field an integrated, layered, ballistic missile defense system (BMDS) to defend the US, its deployed forces, allies, and friends against all ranges of enemy ballistic missiles in all phases of flight.

(1) Missile defense technology being developed, tested, and deployed by the US is designed to counter ballistic missiles of all ranges—short, medium, intermediate, and long. Since ballistic missiles have different ranges, speeds, size, and performance characteristics, BMDS is an integrated, layered architecture that provides multiple opportunities to destroy missiles and their warheads before they can reach their targets. The system's architecture includes networked sensors and ground- and sea-based radars for target detection and tracking; ground- and sea-based interceptor missiles for destroying a ballistic missile using either the force of a direct collision, called "hit-to-kill" technology, or an explosive blast fragmentation warhead; and a command, control, battle management, and communications network providing the warfighter with the needed links between the sensors and interceptor missiles.

(2) Missile defense elements are operated by US military personnel from USSTRATCOM, United States Pacific Command, United States Northern Command, United States Central Command, United States European Command, and others. The US has missile defense cooperative programs with a number of allies, including the United Kingdom, Japan, Australia, Israel, Denmark, Germany, Netherlands, Czech Republic, Poland, Italy, and many others. The MDA also actively participates in NATO activities to maximize opportunities to develop an integrated NATO ballistic missile defense capability.

f. **Air Force Weather Agency.** A field operating agency and the lead weather center of the United States Air Force, AFWA enhances the combat capability of the US by delivering timely, accurate, and reliable environmental situational awareness worldwide to the Air Force, Army, joint warfighters, CCMDs, the IC, and SecDef. AFWA Space Weather Operations Center provides real-time monitoring and forecasting of solar and near-Earth space weather events that impact military operations to the DOD. AFWA is the POC for all DOD and IC space weather information. NOAA's SWPC supports AFWA by providing research and technique development capabilities to improve space weather science for military operations. Additionally, AFWA is a leader in military meteorology. It fields high quality weather equipment and training to Air Force operational weather squadrons and weather flights at locations around the world. AFWA builds a comprehensive weather database of forecast, climatological, and space weather products. These products and services are exploited by military commanders and decision makers for many types of military operations.

13. Commercial Space Operations

a. The commercialization of space supports a growing demand for technologies, services, and products which are commonplace in households, businesses, agencies, and governments on a global scale. Users of space-based products enjoy a wide range of products and services, including global positioning data, satellite radio, direct-to-home television, and even imagery-based products. Businesses and governments at all levels benefit from commercial space operations. Agriculture, fisheries, and geophysical services are among industries that benefit. Emerging services, such as space-based transportation and space-based tourism, are no longer out of reach. Due to the demand for space-based products and services, the USG has established policy to foster the use of US commercial space capabilities around the globe. These capabilities include:

(1) **Commercial Satellite Communications.** Commercial SATCOM are a critical part of US military operations, and planning should include protection of these services. DISA is the only authorized provider of commercial SATCOM for DOD.

See JP 6-0, Joint Communications System, *and CJCSI 6250.01,* Satellite Communications, *for more information.*

(2) **Environmental Monitoring.** Commercial satellites provide remote sensing information. Meteorological satellites and various weather agencies provide additional and redundant capability to US systems. Additionally, many scientific and experimental satellites contribute information on the space environment and terrestrial monitoring. See Appendix C, "Space-Based Environmental Monitoring Capability," for more information.

(3) **Positioning, Navigation, and Timing.** US space-based PNT capabilities are, by Title 10, USC, Section 2281 and national policy, dual military-civilian use. GPS is available to commercial and civilian users and has become the PNT system of choice for US and international applications such as commercial shipping, safety of life, timing of commerce activities, and commercial aviation. The US is committed to improving current GPS capabilities to enhance today's PNT capabilities for both military and civil user

communities. See Appendix E, "Space-Based Positioning, Navigation, and Timing," for more information.

(4) **Commercial Satellite Imagery.** Space-based imagery provided by commercial entities has become an important capability for civil and military operations. Commercial satellites provide electro-optical, infrared, and synthetic aperture radar imaging. Companies can provide imagery, cartography, basic analysis, vessel tracking data, and much more. The joint force obtains these products through NGA just like they would for products from US capabilities. In general, the benefits of these products are that they are readily obtainable, they may free up national systems for higher priority tasks, they can have high resolution, and they are relatively inexpensive. Because these products are unclassified, US forces often share them with multinational and HN members.

(5) **Human Space Flight.** Space-based transportation and tourism will be critical to future competition and development of space-related equipment, components, and procedures. The National Space Policy incorporates maintaining and integrating space capabilities to support civil space agencies.

b. Commercial satellites present capabilities that military commanders may draw on to support planning, operations, and even morale and welfare of the fighting force. However, commercial space operations present unique challenges. Although commercial space capabilities may provide services, they lack assured access and timeliness because capabilities used by US forces are also used by adversaries. Military commanders may request satellite "surge" capabilities while providing DSCA during natural disasters, yet commercial vendors may require long lead time and multiyear leasing to gain access to a capability. Finally, using commercial satellites for military operations presents additional legal issues which must be considered.

c. Even though these challenges exist, military use of commercial capabilities has dramatically increased due to requirements surpassing MILSATCOM resources. To help meet the increased demand, many commercial satellite product vendors have established government services and solutions branches within their organizations to coordinate usage requirements with DOD and other USG departments and agencies. Although these relationships may be largely transparent to military field commanders, the products they request may be eventually fulfilled by a commercial application. In any case, requests for space-based products and services follow standard channels through established procedures.

d. Use of commercial services enhances the resilience of our space enterprise, potentially mitigating the benefits an adversary might gain by attacking US space systems, and by assuring joint forces can operate effectively even when DOD space-derived capabilities have been degraded, disrupted, or destroyed. By enhancing resilience of space capabilities, commercially provided space services enhance deterrence by encouraging adversary restraint in interfering with or attacking those often multiuse, multinational systems.

14. Multinational Space Operations

a. Multinational space operations provide the joint force many opportunities, including increasing interoperability with and extending battlefield advantages to allies, demonstrating responsible behavior in space, and reassuring allies of our commitments to mutual defense. Partnerships can enhance collective security capabilities and can provide a deterrent effect against adversaries from attacking or interfering with friendly space capabilities. Space capabilities derived from a mix of DOD, commercial, multinational, and allied platforms enhance the resilience of our space enterprise and increase the ability of joint forces to operate effectively through a degraded, disrupted, or denied space environment.

b. The NATO Alliance has integrated several space capabilities and established offices which coordinate specific programs for NATO. Supreme Headquarters Allied Powers Europe oversees most programs, such as coordinating with USSTRATCOM for the shared early warning (SEW) system. The NATO Consultation, Command and Control Board oversees the Consultation, Command and Control Agency which is responsible for NATO's commercial space imagery and SATCOM programs.

c. For most other nations, the civilian and commercial segments dominate space operations. Therefore, civilian space agencies have often taken the leadership role for space. Agencies such as the European Space Agency, the United Kingdom Space Agency, the Japan Aerospace Exploration Agency, France's Centre National d'Etudes Spatiales, and the Indian Space Research Organization often issue national policies and strategies in which military space operations may not be addressed. There are allied space operations centers, such as the European Union Satellite Centre, and several others, but they are not typically part of military forces. However, there may be agreements and procedures in place for them to support military operations.

d. US forces rely extensively on foreign environmental satellite capabilities to augment DMSP data. Foreign geostationary environmental satellite data is essential for military operations in Europe and Asia, and in the western-Pacific and Indian Oceans.

e. Multinational forces (MNFs) will have many of the same requirements for space services and capabilities as do US forces. However, US foreign disclosure policy will dictate the nature and scope of disclosure and release of space-derived products to multinational partners. Commercial imagery products are normally unclassified and will be of great benefit to multinational partners. Weather data is also readily available to share, as is GPS navigation support. Of special importance is the provision for missile warning and defense against attack from ballistic missiles. USSTRATCOM is responsible, as part of an interagency process and in coordination with GCCs, for assisting in development of missile warning architectures and providing this information to MNFs in a process called SEW.

See JP 3-16, Multinational Operations, *for additional information.*

15. Other Space-Related Support

a. **Defense Support of Civil Authorities.** Natural or man-made disasters and special events can temporarily overwhelm local, tribal, state, and non-DOD federal responders.

DOD has a long history of supporting civil authorities in the wake of catastrophic events. SecDef may approve requests from civil authorities or qualifying entities for military support. In addition, under imminently serious conditions and if time does not permit approval from higher authority, DOD officials may provide an immediate response by temporarily employing the resources under their control to save lives, prevent human suffering, and mitigate great property damage within the US. DSCA is performed within the parameters of the National Response Framework.

(1) The space assets/capabilities available for DSCA include satellite imagery, overhead persistent infrared (OPIR), FFT, environmental monitoring, SATCOM, and GPS.

(2) Although traditionally an intelligence mission, space personnel can assist with DSCA by helping acquire commercial satellite imagery. The value of this imagery is that it is unclassified, and can be shared with multiple agencies and partner nations. Available sources of commercial imagery include both military sources and commercial vendors. A satellite imagery source specifically put in place for foreign humanitarian assistance is the International Charter Space and Major Disasters. In addition, the SCA can request support (through USSTRATCOM) from an Army space commercial imagery team to provide directly downlinked commercial satellite imagery, commercial imagery spectral analysis, and custom mapping products.

For additional information, see JP 3-28, Defense Support of Civil Authorities.

b. **Information Operations.** The integrated employment during military operations, of information-related capabilities in concert with other lines of operation (LOOs) to influence, disrupt, corrupt, or usurp the decision making of our adversaries and potential adversaries while protecting our own.

(1) Commanders should plan to fully integrate IO into their operations, to include how space-based capabilities can support IO. It is vital that IO and space representatives coordinate their efforts through an IO cell. The IO cell brings all capabilities, to include special technical operations, into the planning cycle to ensure the commander's objectives are achieved. Planners need to coordinate and synchronize space control with IO portions of plans to include which desired effects can be created by space forces or other information-related capabilities. Effective synchronization will prevent negative impacts to IO portions of plans.

(2) IO can benefit greatly from global communication, reachback support, timing, and global synchronization. IO planners should coordinate with the SCA to cue space assets to recognize key events or triggers if they are needed to initiate IO portions of plans.

(3) Space forces have active and passive capabilities (collecting, controlling, exploiting, and protecting information) that can support joint force efforts to conduct military operations.

(4) Space planners need to be integrally involved with IO planners in the planning process as a member of the IO cell to ensure that redundant links and appropriate bandwidth are available to accomplish rapid and reliable global communication.

(5) Some of the ways space-based capabilities can support information-related capabilities in the field are providing two-way secure communications in remote areas, imagery of an operational area, position and navigation information, ISR, and weather, terrain, and environmental monitoring.

See JP 3-13, Information Operations, *for additional information.*

c. **Cyberspace Operations.** The physical domains (air, land, maritime, and space) and information environment rely on cyberspace for instant communications, but the linkages between space and cyberspace are of particular importance as space provides a global connectivity option for CO. In addition, cyberspace provides the means by which space control and transmission of space sensor data are conducted. These interrelationships are critical, and the linkages must be addressed during all phases of joint operation planning.

See JP 3-12, Cyberspace Operations, *for additional information.*

d. **Purposeful Interference Response Team (PIRT).** The USG considers PI with its space systems as an infringement on its rights. PI consists of deliberate actions taken to deny or disrupt a space system, service, or capability. The PIRT is led by DOD through USSTRATCOM and brings together representatives from the USG to include the Departments of Defense, State, Commerce/National Telecommunications and Information Administration (NTIA), Homeland Security, and Transportation/Federal Aviation Administration; the Federal Communications Commission; CSAs and other selected centers of the IC; and the SCAs of the geographic CCMDs. The PIRT is designed to provide an interagency forum to evaluate the impact of suspected PI on US national interests, and provide coordinated, interagency options to resolve them.

CHAPTER V
PLANNING

> *"Planning begins with the end state in mind, providing a unifying purpose around which actions and resources are focused."*
>
> **Joint Publication 5-0, *Joint Operation Planning***

1. General

a. Commanders address space operations in all types of plans and orders, at all levels of war. Additionally, plans must address how to effectively integrate capabilities, counter an adversary's use of space, maximize use of limited space assets, and to consolidate operational requirements for space capabilities.

(1) The GCC may request CDRUSSTRATCOM's assistance in integrating space forces, capabilities, and considerations into each phase of campaign and major OPLANs.

(2) Joint force planners incorporate space forces and capabilities into the basic plan and the applicable annexes (e.g., A, B, C, H, J, K, L, M, N, S, and V, at a minimum).

(3) During mission analysis, planners assist the CCDR to identify specified, implied, and essential tasks for space forces. Additionally, the adversary's capabilities, including their ability to impact our space forces and their use of space capabilities, are considered in JIPOE. Finally, military planners identify those space forces and capabilities that are potential adversary or friendly centers of gravity (COGs), or are critical parts of COGs.

(4) In staff estimates, the planners examine their functional specialties to identify the role and contributions of space forces in the various phases of the joint operation or campaign. During preparation of the commander's estimate, space forces and capabilities are war gamed along with other forces to allow the JFC to make an informed decision.

(5) The completed plan should describe how space operations support the commander's stated objectives, how the adversary employs its space forces, the process and procedures through which additional support will be requested.

(6) The JFC should plan for joint forces to operate in and through a degraded, disrupted, or denied space environment. Planners should consult space or functional experts to discern which capabilities will not be available during the operation. The completed plan should describe how the commander will execute the plan in the event space capabilities are degraded, disrupted, or denied. Planning should consider mission assurance options such as requesting rapid restoration of space assets and leveraging allied, foreign, and/or commercial space and non-space capabilities to help assure mission success.

(7) Space forces can also be used to support or conduct flexible deterrent options (FDOs). Conducting a ballistic missile defense exercise with US allies is one possible FDO

if the CCDR is facing a ballistic missile threat. Another FDO could be to publish, in the world media, high-resolution images from commercial satellites and other systems to clearly demonstrate the adversary's preparations for war and to raise public awareness.

(8) **Annex N (Space Operations)** provides detailed information on space forces and their capabilities that the supported commander can use throughout the joint operation or campaign. The format for annex N is found in Chairman of the Joint Chiefs of Staff Manual (CJCSM) 3130.03, *Adaptive Planning and Execution (APEX) Planning Formats and Guidance*. Annex N directly relates to those space capabilities included in other places such as annex A (Task Organization), annex B (Intelligence), appendix 3 (Information Operations) to annex C (Operations), annex H (Meteorological and Oceanographic Operations), annex J (Command Relationships), annex K (Communications Systems), annex L (Environmental Considerations), annex M (Geospatial Information and Services), annex S (Special Technical Operations), and annex V (Interagency Coordination).

b. **Coordination.** Coordination of space operations between the staffs of the supported and supporting commanders is normally established through the designation of an SCA. The designated SCA coordinates the identification of operational requirements and their inclusion in the appropriate annex. The result of this process is a supportable, valid statement of requirements that can be used by the supporting commander.

(1) During coordination, the operational requirements are evaluated to identify shortfalls in capability, appropriate use of space forces, compliance with national policy, and feasibility of mission success.

(2) When shortfalls or other limitations are identified, they are forwarded to SecDef via the CJCS for further coordination, resolution, adjudication, and apportionment.

c. **Supporting Plans.** USSTRATCOM components develop supporting plans as required. Consideration is given to, and balanced with, requirements of all supported joint force space users.

(1) The Joint Staff evaluates requirements based on priority of use, alternative solutions, impact of loss, and SecDef or CJCS guidance. The review and approval of the supporting plan are the responsibility of the supported commander.

(2) If the supporting commander cannot meet the supported commander's requirements because of planning commitments previously granted to other commanders or agencies, the CJCS or SecDef will adjudicate and resolve the conflicting requirements.

2. Operational Art and Operational Design

a. Since operational art integrates ends, ways, and means across the levels of war, operational art and operational design should be considered when planning space operations at all levels. A mix of DOD commercial, multinational, and allied space capabilities can support or enable operational art and operational design. They are a means to achieve the required end, or a way to support or enable other means to achieve the required end. As such, space forces and capabilities must be considered equally with forces and capabilities throughout the OE.

For additional information on operational art and operational design, see JP 3-0, Joint Operations, and JP 5-0, Joint Operation Planning.

b. Operational design is characterized by the following fundamental elements:

(1) **Termination.** Knowing when to terminate military operations and how to preserve achieved advantages is a component of strategy and operational art and operational design. Space-based ISR supports the JFC's general situational awareness by enabling understanding of when to terminate operations. Space-based ISR can also persistently monitor situations in support of stability operations or treaty obligations.

(2) **Military End State.** Once the termination criteria are established, operational design continues with development of the military end state and conditions based on the national strategic end state. Since space operations are usually in support of other operations, the end state is not usually space specific.

(3) **Objectives.** Once the military end state is understood and termination criteria are established, operational design continues with development of strategic and operational military objectives. Objectives and their supporting effects provide the basis for identifying tasks to be accomplished. Depending on the operation or campaign, there may be space specific objectives; but there will always be a requirement for space support to military operations in support of other objectives of the operation or campaign.

(4) **Effects.** Identifying desired and undesired effects within the OE connects military strategic and operational objectives to tactical tasks. Determining specific desired and undesired effects in relation to space operations can help commanders and their staffs gain a common picture and shared understanding of the OE that promotes unified action.

(5) **Centers of Gravity.** The essence of operational art lies in being able to mass the effects of combat power against the enemy's sources of power in order to destroy or neutralize them. COGs are those characteristics, capabilities, or locations from which a military force derives its freedom of action, physical strength, or will to fight. Given our dependency on space capabilities, space assets should be considered a COG for the JFC. Space assets are also important in helping to identify enemy COGs.

(6) **Decisive Points.** By correctly identifying and controlling decisive points, a commander can gain a marked advantage over the enemy and greatly influence the outcome of an action. For example, decisive points for the assured access to space are launch complexes and ground stations.

(7) **Lines of Operation and Lines of Effort.** As JFCs plan the operation they may use multiple LOOs and/or lines of effort. Generally, LOOs describe the linkage of various actions on nodes and/or decisive points with an operational or strategic objective. A line or effort links multiple tasks and missions using the logic of purpose—cause and effect—to focus efforts toward establishing operational and strategic conditions. Lines of effort are

often essential to helping the commander visualize how military capabilities can support the other instruments of national power. Inasmuch as space operations support most operations, LOOs and lines of effort may be a factor during space planning.

(8) **Direct and Indirect Approaches.** In theory, direct attacks against enemy COGs are the most direct path to victory. However, where direct attack means attacking into an opponent's strength, JFCs should seek an indirect approach. If space-enabled C2 is an adversary's COG, then OSC is an example of a direct approach against the space component of the adversary's C2 COG. If public support for military operations is an adversary's COG, then the use of SATCOM to deliver IO messages is an example of an indirect approach against an adversary's COG.

(9) **Anticipation.** JFCs should remain alert for the unexpected and for opportunities to exploit the situation. Space-borne ISR fused into the COP supports the JFC's overall situational awareness and improves his ability to exploit unexpected opportunities. The predictive attributes of SSA are key to the anticipation of threats to space systems. A JFC anticipates and plans for the loss of space systems or capabilities through regular exercises.

(10) **Operational Reach.** Operational reach is the duration and distance across which a unit can successfully employ military capabilities. Since national boundaries do not extend into space, satellites may provide the timeliest access to denied areas.

(11) **Culmination.** Culmination has both an offensive and defensive application. In the offense, the culmination occurs at the point in time and space at which an attacker's combat power no longer exceeds that of the defender. A defender reaches culmination when the defending force no longer has the capability to go on the counteroffensive or defend successfully. Attacking an enemy's C2 structure through OSC operations can reduce their combat power and lead to earlier culmination. Conversely, loss of critical space capabilities could lead to unanticipated early culmination for the JFC.

(12) **Arranging Operations.** JFCs must determine the best arrangement in the execution of operations. This arrangement will often be a combination of simultaneous and sequential operations to achieve the desired end state quickly and at the least cost in personnel and other resources. When best to employ space capabilities, particularly during offensive operations, is a key concern for the JFC. Space-based sensors can provide details of geography of the operational area, thereby supporting planning and arranging of operations. In phasing operations, planners should consider the footprint, visibility, and signal strength of available space-based capabilities (e.g., GPS accuracy and OPIR).

(a) **Simultaneity and Depth.** The intent of simultaneity and depth is to bring both military and nonmilitary power to bear concurrently across the tactical, operational, and strategic levels of war, to overwhelm the adversary across multiple domains, thus disrupting the opponents decision cycle causing failure of their moral and physical cohesion. PNT and SATCOM enable precision operations on a global scale and can be optimized to provide capabilities anywhere within a theater, or within multiple theaters. Additionally, space force enhancement contributes to the establishment and maintenance of a space COP, which is critical to carrying out simultaneity and depth in joint operations.

(b) **Timing and Tempo.** The joint force should conduct operations at a tempo and time that best exploits friendly capabilities and inhibits the enemy. With proper timing, JFCs can dominate the action, remain unpredictable, and operate beyond the enemy's ability to react. For instance, the employment of OSC capabilities against adversary communications can inhibit the enemy's timing and tempo.

(13) **Forces and Functions.** Commanders and planners plan campaigns and operations that focus on defeating either enemy forces or functions, or a combination of both (see JP 3-0, *Joint Operations,* for a discussion of joint functions). Space control focuses on defeating adversary efforts to interfere with or attack US or allied space systems while enhancing our own.

For additional information on the elements of operational design, see JP 3-0, *Joint Operations,* and JP 5-0, *Joint Operation Planning.*

3. Key Planning Considerations

a. Space presents unique planning and operational considerations that affect friendly, adversary, and neutral space forces alike. Space capabilities require extensive and advanced planning. Space assets are sufficiently capable and robust; however, operational planners must understand the limited number of resources available and the distinct challenges with space force reconstitution. Numerous resource and legal considerations impact planning and affect mission success. The space planner understands planning and operational considerations for employment of space capabilities, and has a firm knowledge of the threats to the use of those systems by an adversary. The space planner must understand what can be done to limit an adversary's use of space capabilities and how to protect our own use of space. Finally, a planner understands how space capabilities relate to and support capabilities and operations throughout the OE.

b. **Global Access.** The fact that there are no geographical boundaries or physical obstructions in space gives military forces global access and extensive advantage.

(1) A single satellite in a low Earth polar orbit will overfly every location on the Earth's surface within a 24-hour period. However, basic orbital mechanics limit the time some satellites can remain over a particular geographic area. The amount of time that a terrestrial AOI will be within a satellite's direct field of view will vary from minutes to years, depending on the satellite orbit type and the field of view of the satellite sensor/antenna (see Appendix G, "Space Fundamentals," for a more in-depth discussion of orbit types and considerations).

(2) With a sufficient number of satellites in appropriate orbits, it is possible to maintain continuous LOS of, and have access to, any points on the surface of the Earth.

(3) Global access is one of the key advantages that space capabilities offer. Most spacecraft can serve multiple users around the world simultaneously (e.g., missile warning satellites).

(4) Despite such global access, however, terrestrial obstructions can affect or limit observations of some points on the Earth from space.

c. **Persistence.** A geostationary orbit allows a satellite to remain over the same area of the Earth 24 hours a day, providing continuous access to a given terrestrial AOI. However, geostationary orbits do not permit high resolution views of high latitude regions. Polar or highly inclined orbits are needed to view these regions, at the cost of reduced dwell time over a given AOI. Because orbits are easily determined, short dwell times and intermittent coverage by a given satellite may provide an adversary significant windows of opportunity for unobserved activity. Therefore, most satellite surveillance systems consist of multiple satellites or be supplemented by other sensors if continuous surveillance of an area is desired.

d. **Limitations** on the operating lifetime of a satellite include the following:

(1) The design life of the satellite.

(2) **Maintenance Considerations.** Physical maintenance currently cannot be performed on most satellites while in orbit. Maintenance is conducted daily using RF digital commands. Satellite maintenance relies on the use of redundant systems, robust design, and alternative subsystems configurations.

(3) As with physical maintenance, on-orbit refueling cannot currently be performed on satellites on orbit, so the amount of fuel carried for changing or maintaining the spacecraft's desired orbit and altitude must be taken into consideration. Satellite orbital maneuvers may be costly in terms of fuel expended. Although some satellite maneuvers can occur quickly (e.g., station keeping), the ability to move a geosynchronous satellite over another part of the Earth may require weeks or months to perform. Satellite maneuvers requiring the use of fuel could shorten the overall useful life of the satellite.

(4) The type of orbit used by the spacecraft.

(5) **Space Weather.** Unexpectedly large or frequent space weather events could shorten a satellite's planned life either by a significant single event or an increased rate of degradation to instruments and systems.

(6) The ever-increasing potential of collisions from other satellites or space debris.

e. **Predictable Orbits.** A satellite's motion or orbital location is predictable, allowing for warning of satellite overflight, maintaining situational awareness, and tracking the location of objects in space. However, there are several forces at work that slowly degrade the predictive accuracy of a satellite's location. These forces will cause a satellite's orbit to slowly change. A satellite may maneuver and change its orbit, making the orbit hard to predict to anyone but the organization initiating the maneuver. However, maneuvering may come at a high cost in terms of onboard fuel, a limited resource. These motion predictions (satellite ephemeris) become less accurate over time and require periodic updates on a daily to weekly basis.

f. **Vulnerability.** All segments of a space system are vulnerable to interference or attack. Space segments are vulnerable to attacks or interference such as direct-ascent anti-satellite interceptors, laser blinding, and dazzling. Additionally, ground-to-satellite link segments are susceptible to jamming and other forms of interference, and ground segments such as C2 facilities are vulnerable to attack. Launch facilities must be protected to ensure access to space so that force replenishment may be accomplished. Some space capabilities may also be subject to exploitation, such as an adversary using commercial GPS receivers for navigation. Knowledge of an adversary's OSC and exploitation capabilities will allow a joint space planner to develop appropriate responses. Space capabilities are also subject to the effects of space weather, including sunspot activity and various types of terrestrial weather. Rain, clouds, fog, and air particulates can interfere with the differing wavelengths used by various satellite functions.

g. **Space Deterrence.** The US employs a variety of measures to deter others from interference and attack on our space systems and those of our allies. DSC capabilities contribute to a multi-layered approach to deterrence, which also includes efforts to promote responsible use of space capabilities and development of partnerships that encourage adversary restraint. Deterrence is also enhanced as we improve our ability to quickly detect, characterize, and attribute attacks. Planners must develop options to deter, defend against, and if deterrence fails, to defeat efforts to interfere with or attack US or allied space systems.

h. **Resource Considerations.** Long lead times to replenish or replace space assets may result in less than adequate space assets to meet a commander's requirements.

(1) Current launch campaigns take weeks to months to generate and execute, provided that all hardware, including payload, is available at the launch site. Payload availability, prelaunch processing, positioning, weather, and on-orbit checkout are factors that can significantly lengthen the time from call-up to operating on-orbit.

(2) Some forces can perform multiple missions. For example, some missile warning sites perform secondary missions of space surveillance and missile defense.

(3) Multiple DOD organizations apportion space capabilities according to established and validated priorities which allow the greatest total mission assurance for the joint force. While there are numerous satellites capable of supporting a requirement, higher priority requirements will be satisfied first.

(4) Users may be preempted based on priority. Competition for bandwidth, priorities for tasking, and similar constraints, combined with satellite physical access to specific locations, impact availability of space capabilities.

i. **Timing Considerations.** SATCOM is heavily dependent on precise timing capabilities. Precise time enables information throughput by increasing the effective use of the bandwidth, and allows for the frequency hopping and cryptographic functions inherent in some communications systems.

(1) According to CJCSI 6130.01, *CJCS Master Positioning, Navigation, and Timing Plan (MPNTP)*, Coordinated Universal Time (UTC) (United States Naval Observatory [USNO]) is the time standard for DOD and the source for time widely disseminated by GPS throughout DOD. However, the vulnerabilities of GPS warrant that communication systems have a backup capability to acquire timing information.

(2) Cryptologic systems and capabilities rely on precise time for synchronization of encrypted communications and information systems. Many communications networks use frequency hopping to improve security and increase resistance to jamming. Therefore, it is essential that planners allow for redundant timing capabilities in the event GPS is disrupted or degraded.

For more information, see CJCSI 6130.01, CJCS Master Positioning, Navigation, and Timing Plan (MPNTP*).*

j. **Legal Considerations.** The joint force complies with US policy and laws, as well as US-ratified treaties and international law, when planning space operations. Legal advisors participate in all stages of space operations planning and execution assessing compliance with applicable legal requirements and providing recommendations as required. There are relatively few legal restrictions on the use of space for military purposes. The US is committed to the exploration and use of outer space by all nations for peaceful purposes, and for the benefit of all humanity. Consistent with this principle, "peaceful purposes" allow US defense and intelligence-related activities in pursuit of national interests.

(1) Some contracts and consortium agreements could prohibit certain space assets from being used for military purposes. For example, certain corporate agreements prohibit using SATCOM for military operations.

(2) The law of armed conflict and certain treaties, acts, and conventions, as they pertain to the use of force, regulation of the means and methods of warfighting, and protection of civilians, must be complied with when conducting space control and space force application operations.

(a) **Treaty on Principles Governing the Activities of States in the Exploration and Use of Outer Space, Including the Moon and Other Celestial Bodies, 1967.** The "Outer Space Treaty" provides that every activity in outer space must be carried out in accordance with international law, including the United Nations (UN) Charter, which recognizes the inherent right of self-defense. All nations are free to use and explore outer space, no nation may appropriate any part of outer space, and every activity in outer space must be carried out with due regard to the corresponding interests of other nations. No nuclear weapon or other weapon of mass destruction may be placed in orbit around the Earth, installed on the Moon or on any other celestial body, or otherwise stationed in outer space. A limited range of military activities, such as establishing bases, weapons testing, and the conduct of military maneuvers, are also prohibited on celestial bodies, to include the

Moon. However, the use of military personnel for scientific research and for any other peaceful purpose is permitted.

(b) **Convention on the Prohibition of Military or Any Other Hostile Use of Environmental Modification Techniques, 1976.** This convention prohibits military or other hostile use of environmental modification techniques as a means of destruction, damage, or injury to the environment (including outer space) if such use has widespread, long-lasting, or severe effects.

(c) **Other Space Treaties.** Other major treaties pertaining to space are the 1968 Agreement on the Rescue of Astronauts, the Return of Astronauts and the Return of Objects Launched into Outer Space (The Rescue and Return Agreement), the 1972 Convention on the International Liability for Damage Caused by Space Objects (Liability Convention), and the Convention on Registration of Objects Launched into Outer Space (Registration Convention) of 1974. The Rescue and Return Agreement obligates nations that have ratified this treaty to cooperate in the rescue and return of distressed personnel of a spacecraft and, upon request of the launching authority, to take those measures it deems practicable to return space objects of other nations that come to Earth within its territory. The Liability Convention provides a system for assessing liability for damage caused by space objects. Generally, a nation is responsible for direct damage caused by a space object to objects on the ground or to aircraft in flight. Damage caused to other space objects, on the other hand, will only lead to liability if one party can establish fault on the part of the other party. Finally, the Registration Convention requires nations to notify the UN "as soon as practicable" after an object has been launched into outer space, providing certain descriptive information, to include orbital parameters and a general statement of the purpose of the space object.

(d) **Noninterference with National or Multinational Technical Means of Verification.** Various arms control treaties prohibit "interference" with national or multinational technical means of verification, i.e., the array of intelligence-gathering capabilities that can be operated from outside the territory of the observed nation in order to monitor the treaty compliance, to include photoreconnaissance satellites and space-based sensors.

(e) **Frequency Spectrum Management.** The International Telecommunications Union governs the allocation of the RF spectrum with all member nations to coordinate frequency assignments and orbital positions of geosynchronous and non-geosynchronous satellite orbits. Individual countries have sovereignty over frequency usage within their borders. Outside of the US, users of any spectrum dependent device, to include space systems, must obtain HN approval to operate those devices in that country. In addition to frequency clearance, users must get landing rights from the HN when operating outside of US territory. These are coordinated through the GCC's joint frequency management office. Within the US, users must obtain frequency clearance from the NTIA through its Service frequency management office for operations in US territory.

(3) In some cases, national policy dictates that space-based capabilities are made available to civilian users. The USG is committed to minimizing impact to peaceful civil use

of GPS outside of the operational area to ensure GPS becomes the space-based navigation capability of choice. JFCs should be aware of this commitment and factor it into NAVWAR planning and OPLANs.

k. **Multinational Space Operations**

(1) Space capabilities have become increasingly important to operations for all nations and NGOs. Access to commercial space services has enabled even the smallest of nations to use GPS, commercial space imagery, SATCOM, and other services. Space capabilities are being used across the range of military operations by our multinational partners and have become a critical enabler for civil and military operations. Currently, the US has the predominance of military space capability; however, many nations are pursuing their own space capabilities. Small satellites also present a very affordable option for many nations. As other nations begin to provide, and have access to, their own (or commercial) space capabilities, the US must seek to partner with responsible nations to provide improved US space capabilities and maintain the strategic advantages we derive from space.

(2) Most nations do not have military space forces and only limited (if any) military space systems. They rely on dual-use satellites and leverage commercial space assets. It is critical to integrate and coordinate the requirements for various national space capabilities and to work releasability issues of US space capabilities in multinational operations. The evolving strategic and fiscal environment allows for additional opportunities to partner with responsible nations, IGOs, NGOs, and commercial firms.

(3) Space is addressed in NATO's Bi-Lateral Strategic Command Functional Planning Guide for Space Operations (NATO Restricted document), and provides guidance for space integration in the operational planning process.

4. **Control and Coordinating Measures**

a. Control and coordinating measures are used by JFCs to provide deconfliction between assets and missions, to maximize efficient and effective use of limited assets, and to provide effective C2 of forces and assets within a defined area. For most DOD space operations, control and coordinating measures are primarily accomplished through applicable guidance from CDRUSSTRATCOM and JFCC SPACE. CDRUSSTRATCOM operations orders provide and assure space capabilities by integrating subordinate component efforts to maintain strategic and operational advantages. In turn, the subordinate components develop supporting plans/directives in support of CDRUSSTRATCOM's guidance to provide synchronized theater and global space capabilities. See Figure V-1.

b. The joint space tasking order development process does not account for missions performed by non-DOD space assets or those limited space forces assigned to a GCC, thereby creating potential conflicts between DOD and non-DOD agencies. It is then incumbent upon the GCCs and JFCC SPACE to coordinate as required to minimize conflicts. To this end, CDRUSSTRATCOM grants JFCC SPACE direct liaison authority with other DOD and non-DOD agencies to help deconflict space operations.

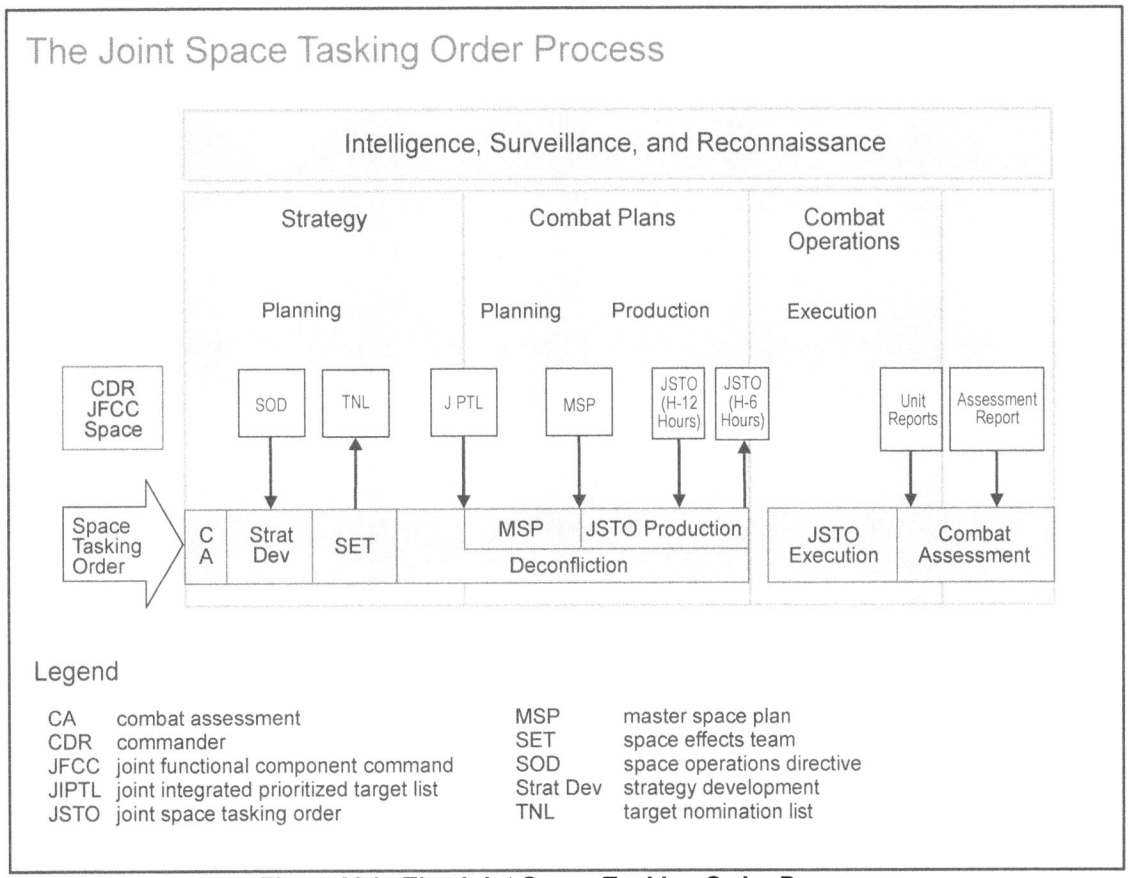

Figure V-1. The Joint Space Tasking Order Process

Intentionally Blank

APPENDIX A
SPACE-BASED INTELLIGENCE, SURVEILLANCE, AND RECONNAISSANCE

1. Overview

Space-based ISR is a part of the synchronization and integration of sensors, assets, PED systems for collection of data and information on an object or in an AOI on a persistent, event driven, or scheduled basis. The JFC and the components have access to space capabilities that can collect diverse military, diplomatic, and economic information that can be valuable for planning and execution across the range of military operations. Specifically, information can be collected, processed, exploited, and disseminated on such diverse subjects as indications and warning (to include ballistic missile launch), targeting analysis, friendly COA development, adversary capability assessment, BDA, or characterization of the OE.

2. Application

a. **Intelligence.** The product resulting from the collection, processing, integration, evaluation, analysis, and interpretation of available information concerning foreign nations, hostile or potentially hostile forces or elements, or areas of actual or potential operations. Space systems contribute to the development of intelligence through surveillance and reconnaissance activities.

b. **Surveillance.** Space systems provide systematic observations of aerospace, surface, or subsurface areas; and places, persons, or things by visual, electronic, photographic, or other means that provide commanders with situational awareness within a given area. Surveillance from space does not imply that a single satellite or capability must be continuously collecting. Satellites that are able to provide a snapshot in time can be augmented by additional capabilities collecting in the same or even different areas of the EMS. There will be short gaps in collection (minutes or a few hours), but capabilities will be concentrating on a target, which, over time, constitutes surveillance. These "following" capabilities can continue collecting on a target as the previous satellite moves out of the area of access in its orbit.

(1) Several satellites in low and medium Earth orbits can provide coverage of targets on the order of minutes. Geosynchronous satellites can provide surveillance because their orbits allow them to have persistent access to large portions of the Earth. Collection from geosynchronous systems may, by necessity, be prioritized based on the area of the world and where within the EMS it can be tasked to collect. In many instances, the number of requirements levied against a system may also necessitate a prioritization of collection. Satellites may also be a contributor to an overall surveillance effort consisting of space, terrestrial, and airborne systems that together provide continuity in surveillance when space systems alone do not have continuous access or are unavailable.

(2) The JSPOC maintains the satellite catalog based upon a global network surveilling on-orbit objects comprised of ground based radar, optical telescopes, and a single space-based optical telescope. This database is used to provide overflight warning to

supported commanders. This database is also used for flight safety to inform satellite operators when satellites are in the path of other man-made orbiting objects.

c. **Reconnaissance.** Reconnaissance is a mission undertaken to obtain, by visual observation or other detection methods, information about activities and resources of an enemy or adversary, or to secure data concerning the meteorological, hydrographic, or geographic characteristics of a particular area. Single low and medium Earth-orbiting systems, or architectures that provide limited numbers of low or medium orbital systems, are well suited to the reconnaissance mission. Generally, their access to specific targets is limited in time based on their orbit such that data collected will be a "snapshot" of events in the portion of the EMS where they can collect. Geosynchronous or geostationary satellites are capable of performing reconnaissance from space as well, focusing their collection efforts on a target or region for a relatively short amount of time before focusing on another area.

3. Advantages

a. The prime advantage of space-based ISR capabilities is their global and wide-area coverage over denied areas where little or no data can be obtained from ground and airborne sources. Other advantages these systems possess include mission longevity and reduced vulnerability to adversary action. While able to provide worldwide coverage, demands on individual space-based systems often exceed their capacity, and their associated orbit requirements may limit the ability to meet operational requirements. Space-based ISR is limited by advanced denial and deception techniques. Space-based systems are owned by military, non-military, and national agencies. International cooperation in military space-based ISR systems with allies and other partners may contribute to US national security objectives by enhancing interoperability, supporting coalition operations, and building partnership capacity.

b. Often, the product of a space or terrestrial capability can enhance accuracy and shorten reaction times to the user by cueing another space system to survey an AOI. Likewise, a space-based capability may be used to cue a terrestrial-based system for more precise location, discrimination, and targeting.

c. ISR systems also enhance planning capabilities by providing updated information regarding terrain and adversary force dispositions. Space-based imagery, in particular, supports the full range of military intelligence activities including indications and warning, current intelligence, order of battle, scientific and technical intelligence assessments, targeting, and combat assessments. Imagery is also used to conduct mission planning and rehearsal.

For additional information on space-based intelligence support, see JP 2-0, Joint Intelligence, and the other JP 2-0 series publications.

4. Limitations

In addition to the access limitations and a predictable overflight schedule dictated by the satellite orbit, satellite systems may be affected by a variety of atmospheric disturbances such as fog, smoke, electrical storms, and precipitation and clouds, which affect the ability of imaging systems to detect adversary activity, missile launches, and battle damage. Other limiting factors include priority conflicts; tasking; PED limitations; and low numbers of assets.

5. **Support Procedures**

a. There are a number of national, military, and nonmilitary space capabilities that can be used individually or in combination to provide the information required by the JFC. The support request procedures for products and information are dependent on the individual system.

See JP 2-01, Joint and National Intelligence Support to Military Operations, *for additional information on national imagery sensors and capabilities.*

b. **National and DOD ISR Support.** National ISR systems provide direct support to the President. The information provided by these systems is used by senior government leaders to make strategic political or military decisions, and is also of great utility to the JFC. Information from national systems is provided to the JFC by direct and indirect feeds in addition to Service component tactical exploitation of national capabilities programs and distributed common ground system elements. Requests for ISR support should go through the intelligence directorate of a joint staff (J-2) and/or the operations directorate of a joint staff at the CCMD or joint force and the J-2 collection manager. Additional sources of information and assistance include the liaison officer, embedded JFCC ISR representative, or support team assigned from the appropriate national or DOD intelligence agencies.

See JP 2-0, Joint Intelligence, *for additional information on fundamental principles and guidance for intelligence support to joint operations and unified action.*

c. **Nonmilitary and Commercial Imagery Support.** National and USG civil imagery satellites provide most of the imagery support to joint operations. However, nonmilitary space surveillance systems (including commercial and allied space capabilities) may augment DOD space systems, enhancing surveillance and reconnaissance coverage of the Earth.

(1) Commercial electro-optical imaging satellites are capable of providing large area, mid-resolution images with a revisit time from 3 to 15 days. Recent increases in the number and quality of commercial imagery satellites provide a valuable opportunity to augment national systems with panchromatic, multispectral, and radar imagery products. All commercial imagery is requested through the NGA.

(2) The greatest limitation of commercial imagery is a lack of understanding in how to use the available systems. Commercial imagery timelines are not adequate to fulfill most stated theater collection requirements with revisit times between 3 and 15 days. Lengthy revisit times and competition will dictate how long a request for imagery takes to fill, which could take up to a year. In times of conflict, these capabilities could provide an advantage to adversaries, since the sale of information from these systems is often not restricted. The sale of commercial imagery to non-USG customers may be interrupted (i.e.,

"shutter control") via the procedures contained in CJCSM 3219.01, *Interruption of Remote Sensing Space System Data Collection and Distribution During Periods of National Security Crisis*.

(3) NGA is the sole DOD action agency for all purchases of commercial and foreign government-owned imagery-related remote sensing data by DOD components. To support this, NGA has established contracts with major commercial imagery vendors.

(4) Before commercial products can be relied upon for targeting and accurate geolocations, they should be verified by NGA. NGA provides this service on a case-by-case basis. Requests for these services must be validated by the appropriate geospatial information and services (GI&S) staff agency at the CCMD or Service component before being forwarded to NGA. Commercial imagery resolution and timeliness may not be adequate to satisfy specific needs.

d. **Geospatial Information and Services Support.** Joint forces receive current and accurate GI&S products from NGA. In addition, NGA can provide supplemental updates to military forces on port conditions, river stages, recent urban construction, vegetation analysis, ice coverage, and oceanographic features. Space-based imagery can provide current information on terrain, surface moisture conditions, oceanic subsurface conditions, beach conditions, and vegetation that permit identification of avenues of approach, specific ingress and egress routes, and other mission parameters to assist in the JIPOE.

(1) Currently, the major source for geospatial data is visible-spectrum imagery provided by national intelligence systems. Imagery provides a detailed overhead view of the area that is analyzed to identify natural and man-made features. Stereo imagery provides elevation data and improved identification of features. Ephemeris and altitude data that accompanies the imagery allows for the precise geodetic positioning of the image and mensuration of features.

(2) Panchromatic, multispectral, and hyperspectral imagery are contributing sources of data for the development and update of GI&S. Satellite systems are vital for

---

OPERATION UNIFIED RESPONSE

During Operation UNIFIED RESPONSE, the International Charter "Space and Major Disasters" and the United Nations Operational Satellite Applications Programme office were instrumental in providing free satellite imagery and finished assessment products to the international humanitarian assistance/foreign disaster relief efforts in Haiti.

In addition to these international resources, Headquarters United States Southern Command created an information portal to share satellite imagery products, full motion video feeds from airborne assets, and finished assessment products with the international community to aid the planning and execution of international relief efforts.

Various Sources

---

providing GI&S data because of their global coverage and periodic updates.

(3) During a crisis, it is important to understand that geospatial information producers are in direct competition with intelligence activities for national collection systems. In some cases, this competition could be mitigated by the use of civil and commercial imagery sources as discussed above.

See JP 2-03, Geospatial Intelligence Support to Joint Operations, *for additional information.*

Intentionally Blank

APPENDIX B
MISSILE WARNING

1. Overview

Missile tracking operations contribute to the ability to provide warning of ballistic missile launches. Voice and data warning information is relayed to the joint force in near real time to support tactical decision making and provide executable data to the missile defense network to counter the threat.

2. Application

a. The missile warning mission uses a mix of space-based and terrestrial sensors. Missile warning includes the notification to national leaders of a missile attack against North America, as well as attacks against multinational partners. It also includes notification to GCCs, multinational partners, and forward deployed personnel of missile attack.

(1) A well-organized missile warning system structure allows commanders to maximize detection and warning of inbound ballistic missiles, thereby ensuring effective passive defense, active defense, and attack operations.

(2) Missile warning systems process raw sensor data into missile warning reports and disseminate the information to users globally. Missile warning consists of multiple ground and space-based systems located worldwide.

b. Space-based sensors, such as Defense Support Program and space-based infrared system, usually provide the first level of immediate missile detection. Some satellite sensors also accomplish nuclear detonation detection. Ground-based radars provide follow-on information on launches and confirmation of strategic attack. The majority of their day-to-day mission is space surveillance; however, the radars are always scanning the horizon for incoming missiles. These ground-based radar systems include the following: Ballistic Missile Early Warning System, PAVE Phased Array Warning System, and the Perimeter Acquisition Radar Attack Characterization System. Upgraded early warning radars are

Space-based and terrestrial sensors play a role in missile detection and warning.

multi-mission radars supporting the missile warning, space surveillance, and the missile defense missions. There is no room for error in missile warning for homeland defense; therefore, all information provided must be timely, accurate, and unambiguous.

For information on performance criteria for missile warning, see CJCSI 6210.02, Information and Operational Architecture of the Integrated Tactical Warning and Attack Assessment System.

c. Because the reaction time for theater forces to respond to incoming missiles is relatively short, GCCs have adopted a strategy known as "assured" warning. This strategy weighs accepting potentially false reports against the time required to obtain unambiguous reports. Under this strategy, the GCCs have elected to receive quicker launch notifications understanding that the warning could be ambiguous. In addition, missile warning elements process raw sensor data from satellite systems, form that data into missile warning reports, and disseminate the information to theater users. Missile warning elements consist of multiple US ground and in-theater units.

d. **Missile Warning Requests.** JFCs should forward requests for missile warning to CDRUSSTRATCOM via approved procedures. (See Figure B-1.)

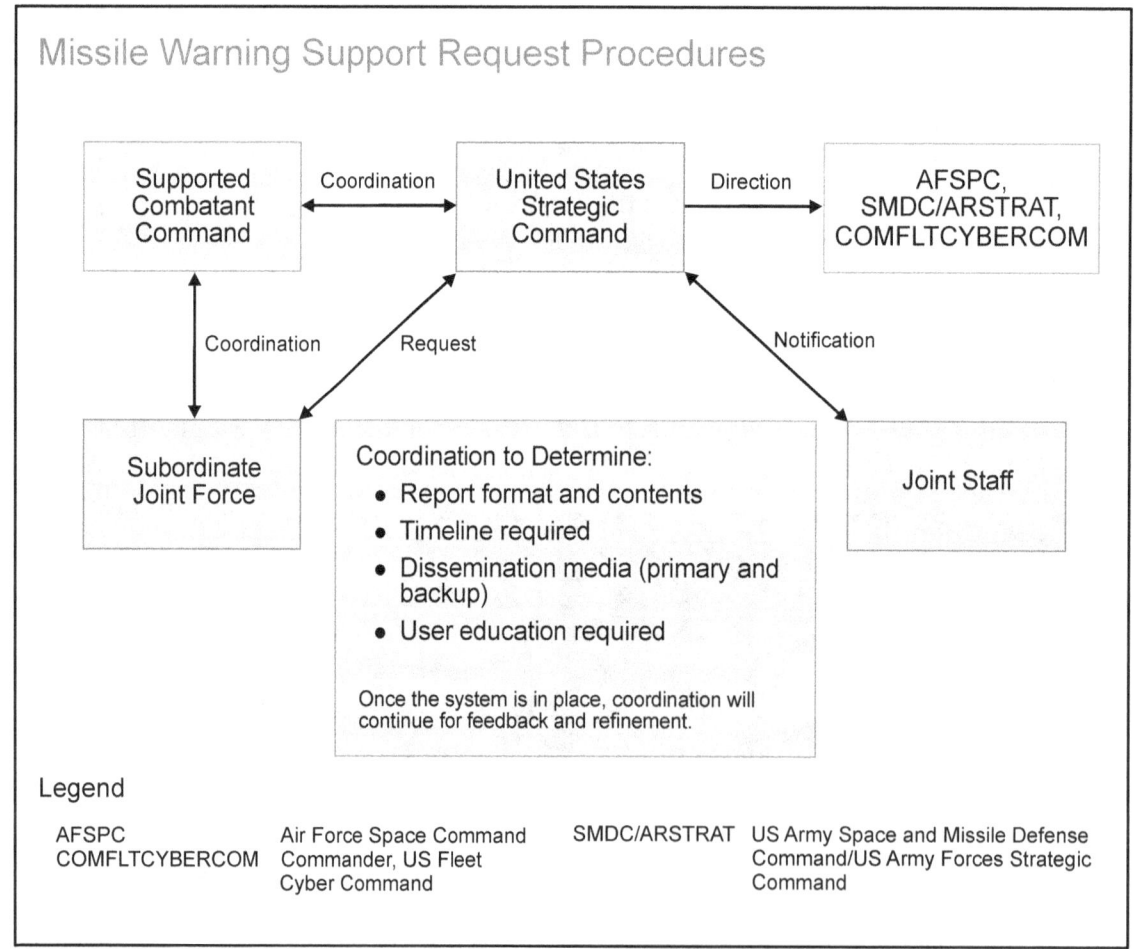

Figure B-1. Missile Warning Support Request Procedures

(1) When requesting support from missile warning elements, users should clearly state their requirements and applicable objectives as appropriate. Requests should include specific threat assessment, location and type of threat, duration of support requested, primary and secondary communications media preferred for reporting, false reporting tolerance, and levels and units within the command structure to which the warning data and information will be provided.

(2) Upon receiving a request, CDRUSSTRATCOM will assess its ability to provide support based on the assets assigned to the command. Once the command has determined a COA, it will provide that feedback through the SCA of the supported command.

e. **Missile Warning Exercise Support**

(1) **Exercise Design.** The theater event system (TES) elements will use operational hardware, software, and procedures to the maximum extent possible for exercises. For each exercise requiring TES support, USSTRATCOM will determine, after taking into account the requirements of the requesting agency, if the TES processor elements or a simulation device will support the exercise. USSTRATCOM will provide the Missile Warning Center, theater, and all participating TES elements, or simulation organizations with the missile launch scenario, the voice reporting architecture, and templates (if different from real-world).

(2) **Exercise Coordination.** Coordination with USSTRATCOM is required prior to TES elements or simulation systems injecting exercise traffic. Request for TES exercise support must be submitted to USSTRATCOM via a consolidated exercise support request. USSTRATCOM will review and approve exceptions on a case-by-case basis, and is responsible to ensure that a user's message is released announcing the exercise specifics.

(3) Dissemination of exercise data over the Integrated Broadcast Service requires separate approval and coordination.

(4) The TES elements must keep exercise and real-world data separate and clearly defined.

f. **Shared Early Warning.** The US exchanges missile detection and warning information with its multinational partners. The objective of SEW is the continuous exchange of missile early warning information derived from US missile early warning sensors and, when available, from the sensors of the SEW partner. Information on missile launches is provided on a near-real-time basis. This information can take the form of data, voice warning, or both. The objective of SEW is to enhance regional stability by providing ballistic missile warning to CCDRs, sponsored partner countries, and NATO allies. GCCs will recommend/sponsor SEW partner countries. DOD policy is to provide continuous, near-real-time, ballistic missile early warning information on regional launches that is of the same high quality and timeliness as the launch warning that would be made available to US forces if operating in the same area at the same time. Currently, the SEW system provides both messages and voice warning to partner countries.

For information on missile defense, see JP 3-01, Countering Air and Missile Threats.

Intentionally Blank

APPENDIX C
SPACE-BASED ENVIRONMENTAL MONITORING CAPABILITY

1. Overview

METOC support from space facilitates the development of forecasts and assessments of environmental impacts on both friendly and adversary military operations. Environmental monitoring satellites, which typically use sun-synchronous, geosynchronous, and Lagrangian orbits (see Appendix G, "Space Fundamentals," for additional information about orbits), as well as some intelligence satellites, provide terrestrial and space environmental monitoring for joint forces. Environmental monitoring information includes data provided by non-DOD satellites, such as NOAA weather and NASA research satellites, which are used by AFWA and Fleet Numerical Meteorology and Oceanography Center (FNMOC) and the Naval Oceanographic Office (NAVOCEANO) to support joint forces and Services.

2. Application

a. **Weather.** The terrestrial and space environment can adversely impact a wide range of space systems and missions. Space-derived meteorological information is crucial to understanding and reacting to the effects of the environment on both space and terrestrial operations. This information helps commanders assess the environmental impacts on both friendly and adversary forces alike and helps to complete operational preparation of the environment. The environment affects almost all aspects of operations. A few examples are mission timing, route selection, target and weapon selection, mode of weapon delivery, communications, reconnaissance, and surveillance.

b. **Oceanography.** Knowledge of the location and characteristics of oceanographic features, such as sea heights, sea surface ice, currents, fronts, and eddies, is essential to all maritime forces. It is especially critical for undersea warfare operations and can be used by commanders to avoid submarine or maritime mine threats. This knowledge can also be used to concentrate forces in an area where an adversary is most likely to be operating, to optimize SAR operations at sea, and to help determine optimum locations for amphibious landings.

c. **Space Environment.** Environmental data from the space domain must be available to integrate into SSA information to form a space COP. This enables joint forces to determine the impact of environmental factors on both adversary and friendly space and weapons systems.

3. Advantages

a. A prime advantage of environmental satellites is their ability to gather data in remote or hostile areas, where little or no data can be obtained via surface reporting stations. For example, space-based environmental data is critical over most oceanic regions, where data can otherwise be very sparse.

b. Environmental satellites typically gather data in the visual, infrared, and microwave spectral bands. Infrared sensors provide images that are based on the thermal characteristics of atmospheric features, such as clouds, and Earth features, such as land masses and water bodies. This data can be used to calculate the altitude of cloud tops and ground or water surface temperatures.

c. Thermal and visible images together provide the coverage and extent of clouds at various levels, as well as other physical features such as ice fields and snow. Current microwave sensors are used to measure or infer sea surface winds (direction and speed), ground moisture, rainfall rates, ice characteristics, atmospheric temperatures, and water vapor profiles.

d. Space-based monitoring of the space domain provides the ability to detect and mitigate the impacts of space weather on satellites, manned spaceflight, and communications to, from, and through space. Detection of solar events and measurement of the radiation environment allow operators to protect resources and deduce likely causes of spacecraft anomalies.

4. Limitations

a. Polar-orbiting satellites have periodic revisit rates over the target area, and therefore have a limited time over target for observations. However, these satellites provide global coverage and high-resolution data at all latitudes.

b. Geosynchronous satellites provide lower resolution images, but maintain a constant view of their coverage area. The image quality of geosynchronous satellites degrades as distance and angle from the point directly under the satellite increase. Coverage at polar latitudes is poor or nonexistent. US owned and operated geostationary environmental satellites are focused on the western hemisphere (the continental US, eastern Pacific, and western Atlantic). Foreign national capabilities are used for the remainder of the globe.

c. Some METOC parameters needed by forecasters for operational support, including heights of cloud bases and visibility restrictions, cannot be accurately determined from environmental satellites. Data from several sources, including surface observations, upper air soundings, and satellite data, are combined to determine these parameters.

d. Due to the magnitude of the space domain, space-based capabilities are limited in their ability to characterize the space environment in all areas, thereby creating gaps in complete situational awareness.

5. Support Procedures

a. METOC support to joint operations is critical to a JFC's awareness of the OE during all types of joint operations and across the full range of military operations. This support is normally provided by METOC forces assigned to one or more of the participating components. When two or more units are involved in a joint operation, coordination of their support is normally accomplished by the joint METOC coordination cell.

See JP 3-59, Meteorological and Oceanographic Operations, *for more information on the organization of METOC forces.*

b. METOC satellite system data is supplied to AFWA, FNMOC, and the NAVOCEANO. These central facilities provide users with real-time and stored environmental satellite cloud imagery, processed products, and satellite information incorporated into other environmental products. Another source of environmental satellite system information for joint operations is direct downlink of environmental satellite data from fixed and deployed mobile ground- and ship-based tactical data processing terminals within the operational area.

c. AFWA is responsible for collecting, processing, and providing space environmental data products to the joint force.

d. Weather satellite system data is distributed via the DODIN.

Intentionally Blank

APPENDIX D
SATELLITE COMMUNICATIONS

> *"Protected {space} communications make possible the ability to command and control forces and support national decision makers in a contested communications environment, including the high end nuclear environment."*
>
> **Lieutenant General Susan J. Helms**
> **Commander, Joint Functional Component Command for Space**
> **11 May 2011**

1. Overview

SATCOM (military, commercial, foreign, and civil) provides global coverage which affords the US and allied national and military leaders with a means to maintain strategic situational awareness and a means to convey their intent to the operational commander responsible for conducting joint operations in a specific area (see Figure D-1). SATCOM also provides critical connectivity for tactical maneuver forces whose rapid movement and nonlinear deployments take them beyond LOS communication. Military forces are dependent on space-based communications systems to access essential information services in the execution of operations. SATCOM systems provide communications that facilitate C2, access for authorized users, survivable communications for Presidential support, nuclear C2, and ISR sensor collection data.

2. Application

a. SATCOM provides a beyond LOS information transport capability. It allows for communications from the highest levels of government to the theater tactical level for all matters, to include operations, logistics, intelligence, personnel, and diplomacy.

(1) It supports a variety of media to include digital video and audio, and standard network data feeds.

(2) SATCOM are space-based communications relay systems consisting of uplinks and downlinks. The frequency band and waveform are two major factors that determine the throughput capacity and the degree of protection and survivability provided to the communications system (anti-jam [AJ], anti-scintillation, low probability of intercept [LPI], and low probability of detection [LPD] capabilities).

(3) The frequency bands over which current MILSATCOM operate are:

(a) UHF for narrowband communications.

(b) Super-high frequency (SHF) for wideband communications.

Military and Commercial Satellite Systems

Protected

EHF Q/Ka-Band
Milstar I/II

- Survivable/protected communications for national leaders and joint force [AJ, LPI, LPD, EMP hardened]
- Crosslinks (no ground relay required)
- Polar
- Protected communications for north polar region (LPI, LPD)

AEHF/Milstar Follow-on

- Greater throughput
- International partners

Wideband

X/Ka-Band

- High data rates for deployed forces and enterprise users DISN enterprise extensions and DISN reachback for deployed forces

DSCS

- X-band only
- Airborne and maritime COTM capability
- Some AJ

WGS

- DSCS follow-on
- X and Ka-bands
- COTM with Ka-band (airborne and maritime)
- Greater throughput
- International partners

Ka-Band
UFO

- GBS Ka payload
- High throughput
- Small antenna
- Smart push-pull data broadcasts

WGS

- WGS – X- and Ka-bands
- Return channel capability with 2-way Ka-band
- Airborne and maritime COTM capability

Narrowband

UHF P/L-Band
UFO

- Lightweight, mobile
- Low data rates/space segment limited
- Supports joint force, INTEL. LOG nets
- DAMA/IW increases user accesses
- No AJ

MUOS

- UFO follow-on
- Global cellular service
- On-demand use
- Support legacy UHF transition
- Greater number of accesses

Commercial

L, S, C, X, Ku, Ka Bands

- Augment MILSATCOM
- Mobile and fixed satellite services
- High throughput
  ○ telemedicine
  ○ CSS
  ○ split-based operations
  ○ video
- Less protection
- Pay for services

Legend

AEHF	advanced extremely high frequency	L	L-band, 1-2 GHz
AJ	anti-jam	LOG	logistics
C	C-band, 3.7-4.2 GHz	LPD	low probability of detection
COTM	communications on the move	LPI	low probability of intercept
CSS	commercial satellite services	MHz	megahertz
DAMA	demand assigned multiple access	MILSATCOM	military satellite communications
DISN	Defense Information System Network	MUOS	Mobile User Objective System
DSCS	Defense Satellite Communications System	P	P-band, 250-500 MHz
EHF	extremely high frequency	Q	Q-band, 33-50 GHz
EMP	electromagnetic pulse	S	S-band, 2-4 GHz
GBS	Global Broadcast Service	SHF	super high frequency
GHz	gigaherz	UFO	ultrahigh frequency (UHF) follow-on
INTEL	intelligence	UHF	ultrahigh frequency
IW	integrated waveband	WGS	Wideband Global Satellite Communications System
Ka	Kurtz-above band, 27-40 GHz		
Ku	Kurtz-under band, 12-18 GHz	X	X-band, 9-12 GHz

Figure D-1. Military and Commercial Satellite Systems

(c) Extremely high frequency (EHF) band is utilized for protected SATCOM through the EHF satellites and their hosted payloads. The EHF satellite constellations, including the military strategic and tactical relay (Milstar) and the AEHF system, are hardened against solar and nuclear radiation. EHF communications are also supported by the EHF payloads hosted on UFO satellites. The EHF waveforms operate in scalable data throughputs and support survivable, secure, protected, and jam-resistant communications.

b. Narrowband SATCOM systems support secure voice and data transmission at relatively low data rates for both mobile and fixed users.

(1) Narrowband communications traditionally support requirements such as emergency action message dissemination between SecDef and CCDRs, force direction messages, tactical C2, low data rate broadcasts, and force report-back message transmission and reception.

(2) Narrowband systems support highly mobile, tactical users. Compact terminal equipment and directional and omnidirectional antennas allow deployed joint forces to quickly and efficiently exchange both voice and data communications.

(3) Narrowband systems include mobile and fixed terminals installed in air, maritime, and ground platforms; command centers and command posts; and missile launch control facilities.

(4) Narrowband communications use UHF frequencies that allow excellent transmission quality through all types of terrestrial weather to small, tactical terminals; however, UHF and EHF frequencies can be totally disrupted by ionospheric scintillation. Additionally, the bandwidth itself is limited and therefore can only achieve data rates in the kilobits-per-second range.

c. Wideband SATCOM supports multichannel, secure voice, and high data-rate communications for C2, crisis management, and intelligence data transfer.

(1) Wideband communications support a range of government, strategic, and tactical users such as the White House Communications Agency, the uniformed services, Department of State, Joint Staff, CCDRs, joint task forces, MNFs, mobile units, unmanned aircraft systems, and other elements as needed.

(2) Wideband SATCOM provides Defense Information Services Network common user information transport and allows the JFC to reach back to other portions of the DODIN. It also supports Nonsecure Internet Protocol Router Network (NIPRNET), SECRET Internet Protocol Router Network (SIPRNET), and Joint Worldwide Intelligence Communications System.

(3) Wideband communication tactical terminals support exercises and the deployed operations requirements of tactical forces for high-capacity, multichannel communications aboard ships and aircraft, as well as in support of ground forces.

d. Protected SATCOM supports survivable voice and data communications not normally found on other systems.

(1) Protected SATCOM provides scalable throughputs over a wide band of spectrum. In a hostile environment where a wideband system could be degraded, protected SATCOM will allow survivable communication, but at a reduced data rate.

(2) Protected SATCOM characteristics, such as narrow beamwidths and the use of frequency hopping technology, provide capabilities such as AJ, scintillation-resistance, LPI, and LPD. Due to these unique capabilities, the use of the protected SATCOM frequency band has often been reserved for the most critical strategic forces and C2 systems.

e. **Commercial Capabilities.** Commercial SATCOM offers another venue to satisfy DOD's rapidly growing information needs. Some wideband services and personal communications services (e.g., satellite phones) are examples of current commercial SATCOM support to strategic and tactical mobile users. Commercial systems currently support much of DOD's predictable, wideband, and fixed SATCOM needs when MILSATCOM is not available. Leasing commercial services also affords faster access to advanced capabilities and services than traditional government research, development, and acquisition programs. However, in an environment where both the US and its potential adversaries will have almost equivalent access to the same advanced technologies and commercial services, sustaining military advantage may largely rest on the US ability to integrate those technologies and commercial services into its force structure faster and more effectively than the adversary. The DOD agencies, Services, and CCMDs procure commercial SATCOM solutions using the Future Commercial Satellite Communications Services Acquisition program, which is an acquisition vehicle managed by DISA.

3. Advantages

The inherent capabilities of satellite systems provide significant advantages over other communications systems.

a. **Global Coverage.** Collectively, SATCOM systems provide global coverage. If required, satellites can provide focused capacity in areas of special interest.

b. **Real-Time Over-the-Horizon Transmission of Voice and Data.** Like other communications media, most SATCOM systems provide real-time connectivity for both voice and data, but unlike other communications media above high frequency, SATCOM can provide over-the-horizon voice and data transmission.

c. **Data Relay.** SATCOM links preclude the need for long terrestrial communications links. Furthermore, SATCOM enables US forces to communicate without substantial terrestrial communications architecture.

d. **Flexibility.** Satellite systems allow global coverage and interlinking between frequency bands and systems, and certain systems are able to provide a relatively LPD. Flexibility gives the JFC a great deal of latitude in mixing and matching satellite systems to meet specific operational requirements. Directional antennas afford LPD; wide bandwidths allow higher data rates; ground stations permit cross patching; and satellite positions make global coverage available.

e. **Support to Mobile Forces.** SATCOM systems can provide the communications required by mobile forces operating over wide areas. This is especially true for those forces that require dynamic C2 when they are on the move.

4. Limitations

SATCOM has the following limitations:

a. **Limited Capacity.** Requirements for SATCOM service worldwide exceed the capacity of current MILSATCOM systems. Through partnering, the DOD supplements SATCOM capabilities with commercial, international, and civil systems.

(1) Due to the number of SATCOM users, the priority of use, and the criticality of information carried over these systems, oversight through requirement validation and adjudication is required at the DOD, Joint Staff, and CDRUSSTRATCOM levels.

(2) Identified requirements are carefully scrutinized through a validation process, resulting in USSTRATCOM apportioning resources for OPLANs with capacity eventually being allocated based on priority and availability.

(3) Within their allocated capacity, CCDRs manage, direct, and control individual networks supporting component air, land, maritime, space, and special operations forces.

b. **Connectivity Limitations.** Limitations on terminals and teleports/gateways are key planning considerations.

(1) SATCOM terminals are designed to operate in specific spectrum bands, across specific satellites, and in specific environments. Thus, SATCOM terminals will have to be selected based on mission, the environment they will be used in, and data needs.

(2) Teleports/gateways are required to gain access into the DODIN. These are finite gateways with limited resources.

(3) Due to the distances traveled on a SATCOM transmission path, significant latency is introduced into the communications link, which can adversely impact some C2 systems and applications which are latency-sensitive. Accelerators and similar hardware and/or software solutions should be considered to aid in mitigating this.

See United States Strategic Command Strategic Instruction (SI) 714-4, Consolidated Satellite Communications (SATCOM) Management Policies and Procedures (C-SMPP), *for additional information on the SATCOM request validation process.*

c. **Orbital Considerations.** Most DOD communications satellites are in geosynchronous orbits over the equatorial plane where they appear to be stationary over a point on the Earth's equator. See Appendix G, "Space Fundamentals," for a description of geosynchronous and geostationary orbits.

(1) A constellation of three geostationary communications satellites equally spaced, or nearly so, can provide near-total Earth coverage between 65 degrees north and south latitude. However, due to signals becoming weak at the edges of coverage, MILSATCOM generally employs a constellation of four satellites to provide adequate worldwide coverage between 65 degrees north and south latitude.

(2) In general, a mixture of geosynchronous and polar satellites are required for full global coverage. A mixture of satellites in low Earth orbit (LEO), medium Earth orbit (MEO), or highly elliptical orbits (HEOs) can also provide global coverage; however, this requires a greater number of satellites in the constellation to accomplish.

d. **Frequency Constraints.** Except in forcible entry situations, the terminal segments associated with space systems are subject to the same HN and NTIA frequency clearance processes as terrestrial radio systems. In addition, frequency bleed-over among antennas must be considered when configuring ground segments (e.g., antenna farms) to ensure self-imposed interference is avoided, not only on radio systems but GPS frequencies as well.

e. **Terminal and Antenna Size.** Because antenna size, frequency, bandwidth, and data rate capacity are interrelated, commanders often must compromise either information flow rate or mobility.

(1) Generally, the higher the frequency (e.g., SHF, EHF), the greater the available signal bandwidth (hertz) and the higher the data rate (bits per second) capacity. Similarly, within these frequency bands, the larger the antenna size, the greater the data throughput, but a SATCOM terminal's mobility is reduced. However, small terminals and antennas are required to minimize the impacts on tactical force mobility and ensure that the many different platforms of the supported forces are suitably integrated in the operational, physical, power, and electromagnetic environments. Hand-held and/or man-pack, maritime, and airborne platforms have especially demanding constraints.

(2) Lower frequency systems have narrower signal bandwidth and lower data rate capacity.

f. **Susceptibility to Jamming and Interference.** All radio receivers, including satellite systems, are susceptible to jamming and interference. Unintentional interference can be as harmful to SATCOM operations as deliberate jamming. Mandatory jamming and interference resolution processes for all JFCs, Services, and agencies are contained in SI 714-5, *Space System Electromagnetic Interference (EMI) Resolution Procedures.*

(1) Narrowband satellites are the most susceptible to both jamming and intercept due to their narrower bandwidth, large antenna beamwidth, and low power. While most commercial satellites have no protection against jamming, military UHF satellites have limited resistance through the use of different modulation schemes and the use of spread spectrum techniques.

(2) Military wideband systems operate at higher frequencies, smaller antenna beamwidths, and wider bandwidth. The narrower antenna beamwidth provides some advantage in jam resistance and intercept versus narrowband systems. For instance, WGS provides greater protection against interference over its commercial counterparts, through active beam shaping, beam steering, and ability to cross-band communications links between X-band and Kurtz-above band.

(3) Military protected systems (i.e., Milstar or AEHF) afford even greater protection through the different techniques possible with wider available bandwidth. However, since the wider bandwidth is used to create added protected features, data rates are actually decreased.

g. **Constellation Reconfiguration.** While the ability to move satellites to reconfigure constellations may be an advantage, there are also significant disadvantages to repositioning satellites.

(1) Most communications satellites currently in service are positioned to provide communications connectivity to a large number of users. Moving any of the primary satellites to a new satellite region could disrupt communications connectivity for this population, and could impair their ability to accomplish their missions. Movement of satellites requires extensive coordination with multiple agencies. The process to move communications satellites is described in SI 714-4, *Consolidated Satellite Communications (SATCOM) Management Policies and Procedures (C-SMPP)*.

(2) Repositioning satellites can take weeks and can consume a significant amount of onboard, station-keeping fuel, thereby reducing the operational life of the satellite.

(3) To offset this limitation, JFCs must identify their SATCOM requirements through the Joint Staff Satellite Communications Database (SDB) according to the latest version of CJCSI 6250.01, *Satellite Communications,* by following the defined process of submissions through the appropriate CCMD. SATCOM is incorporated into OPLANs as described in SI 714-4.

h. **Solar Activity.** Increased solar activity can disrupt SATCOM for short periods of time. In extreme cases, this can cause communications outages.

(1) Sun activity causes atmospheric scintillation that mostly affects small receivers in the Arctic and tropical regions operating in the UHF frequency band.

(2) The detection of solar flares can be used to forecast solar effects, thereby minimizing the disruption of communications by using workarounds.

(3) All SATCOM is susceptible to solar activity.

i. **Interference Due to Precipitation.** SATCOM in the Kurtz-under and Kurtz-above bands, and EHF systems, are particularly affected by precipitation (the higher the frequency, the greater the effect). Precipitation not only degrades the signal but, if heavy enough, can cause a complete outage. While the percentage of time a system will not be available due to precipitation is small, this is an operational constraint which must be considered during planning or operations.

j. **Sun Conjunctions.** Sun conjunctions (in this context, when a satellite is aligned between the Earth and sun) cause communications disruptions and outages. Since their time and duration can be predicted, such events can be planned for and the impact on operations minimized.

k. **Considerations for Military Use of Commercial SATCOM Systems.** Access to commercial SATCOM systems raises several issues which must be considered:

(1) Communications are not protected.

(2) Potential competition for access with other customers, including adversaries.

(3) Non-US ownership or control of commercial SATCOM services outside the borders of the US.

(4) The potential inability to quickly access commercial SATCOM capacity in many areas to which the military could deploy (often on a short notice).

(5) Access and availability to commercial services are based on contractual terms which could be terminated at times not convenient to the military.

(6) Potential for commercial SATCOM unencrypted TT&C links and lack of vendor ability to identify, geolocate, and support DOD jamming or interference response.

(7) Acquisition of commercial SATCOM may have time constraints and should be considered. Additional time may be required if the vendor must obtain landing rights to operate and HN approval for frequencies from a foreign country.

l. **National Systems for Communications.** In some cases, specialized DOD communications needs can be met through national systems. As with MILSATCOM systems, these assets may be highly subscribed, and therefore require careful coordination and planning with national systems operators before military use can be ensured.

5. **Support Procedures**

The SATCOM requirements process is defined in CJCSI 6250.01, *Satellite Communications*. A summary of the process is provided below.

a. **Requirements Process.** The ultimate objective for SATCOM management is to provide the right users SATCOM resources when and where needed, in accordance with operational priorities. DOD needs to continually assess the SATCOM systems' effectiveness in pursuit of this objective.

(1) The Joint Staff, CCMDs, Services, and DOD agencies are all key stakeholders with MILSATCOM requirements. CDRUSSTRATCOM, per the UCP, serves as the

advocate for DOD operational SATCOM matters, representing the DOD SATCOM community by coordinating and orchestrating consolidated user positions with CCMDs, Services, and agencies.

(2) Each GCC will consolidate, validate, and prioritize all requests for use of SATCOM systems within their AOR.

(3) CCMDs and Services will validate their requirements and submit them to the Joint SATCOM Panel, co-chaired by the Joint Staff and USSTRATCOM.

(4) DOD agencies will validate and submit requirements in support of their agency mission and/or function to the Joint SATCOM Panel, co-chaired by the Joint Staff and USSTRATCOM.

(5) Assistant Secretary of Defense (Networks and Information Integration) is responsible for non-DOD and federal agency requirements.

b. **Format.** SATCOM requirements for user connectivity will be submitted via the SDB Management Tool or via DISA Form 772, *SDB Requirement Request Form.* Current and future requirements will be submitted with the format described in the DISA-published SDB Management Tool user guide.

c. **Prioritization.** CCMDs, Services, and DOD agencies review each requirement to ensure that it is valid, has a clear operational concept, identifies the operational needs and missions supported, and provides a mission impact if not satisfied. The requirements are then prioritized by category as prescribed and documented in CJCSI 6250.01, *Satellite Communications.*

d. **Submission.** All SATCOM (military and commercial) requirements are submitted to the Joint Staff through the joint satellite communications panel administrator (JSPA) at DISA who administers the SDB.

e. **Future Requirements.** Future connectivity requirements are satisfied through ongoing changes to strategy, doctrine, forces, weapon systems, or changes in technology. The SDB consolidates future SATCOM requirements to assist planners in determining future SATCOM capabilities, trends, architectures, and acquisition strategies.

f. **SATCOM Access.** Access is requested via the SATCOM allocation process described in SI 714-4, *Consolidated Satellite Communications (SATCOM) Management Policies and Procedures (C-SMPP).* Lengthy lead times necessitate early planning for a satellite access request or gateway access request (GAR). Terminals identified in the satellite access request or GAR must be certified to operate on DOD satellites, have approval to connect to the DODIN, COMSEC keymat, and have HN-approved frequencies if operating in a foreign country.

g. **Adjudication.** Per CJCSI 6250.01, *Satellite Communications,* the CJCS has final adjudication authority for competing DOD SATCOM access requirements that cannot be resolved by CDRUSSTRATCOM.

h. **Urgent Requirements.** For urgent requirements not documented in the SDB, a request is submitted to USSTRATCOM, with information copies to JSPA. Urgent requirements can be submitted by CCDRs, Service Chiefs, and the directors of DOD agencies, but they must be validated as an operational necessity. The request must contain justification for urgent processing. For urgent requirements, the Joint Staff can grant a 30-day waiver for SDB approval.

See JP 6-0, Joint Communications System, *for keystone communications doctrine.*

APPENDIX E
SPACE-BASED POSITIONING, NAVIGATION, AND TIMING

1. Overview

a. Space-based PNT systems, in combination with terminal units, support strategic, operational, and tactical missions by providing the joint force with essential and precise three-dimensional position capability navigation options, and a highly accurate time reference. US military forces use GPS for their space-based PNT information.

b. In conducting joint military operations, it is essential that PNT services be available with the highest possible confidence. PNT services must meet or exceed JFC mission requirements. Any information that makes reference to time must be able to provide that time in terms of the standard temporal reference defined by UTC as maintained by the USNO master clock, which is the standard for all military systems.

c. GPS satellites broadcast navigation information on a continuous basis. The transmission has two levels of service—a standard positioning service (SPS) and a precise positioning service (PPS). The positioning code in each permits very precise matching of receiver-generated and satellite-generated waveforms, hence, precise measurement of the distance to each satellite.

(1) SPS, which utilizes the coarse acquisition code, is the unencrypted civilian positioning and timing service that is provided to all GPS users.

(2) PPS is a more accurate, military positioning, velocity, and timing service available to authorized encrypted users (e.g., US military and some allies) on a worldwide basis with limited AJ capabilities. Access to PPS is controlled by use of cryptography (encryption keys loaded in the terminal units).

d. **DOD Policy for Precise Positioning Service.** In 2005, Congress directed that all DOD aircraft, ships, combat vehicles, and indirect-fire weapon systems must be equipped with a GPS receiver. However, certain federal civil agencies and multinational members are also authorized use of the PPS through department-level special agreements. GPS policy is included in the DOD GPS Security Policy, DODD 4650.05, *Positioning, Navigation, and Timing,* and CJCSI 6130.01, *2007 CJCS Master Positioning, Navigation, and Timing Plan (MPNTP);* each requires all DOD assets to use a common precise time: UTC (USNO), the standard geospatial reference frame defined by the World Geodetic System 1984 (WGS-84) provided by NGA, and a common precise celestial reference frame (provided by USNO).

(1) Only DOD-approved PNT systems (e.g., inertial navigation system and GPS PPS) will be used for combat, combat support, and combat service support operations. Exceptions to this policy are approved according to the MPNTP.

(2) GPS is the primary source of PNT information for the DOD. Civil capabilities are permitted for use in peacetime operations when the use of the system does not jeopardize the ability to accomplish the US military mission.

(3) All DOD combatant users must acquire, train with, and use GPS PPS systems in accordance with the DOD GPS Security Policy and the MPNTP.

2. Application

GPS plays a key role in military operations by enabling precise location and navigation in all four physical domains (land, maritime, air, and space) and by providing precise timing in cyberspace. GPS capabilities are increasing across the space, control, and user segments (see Figure E-1). In addition to the precise location, navigation, and accurate timing, some of the applications include:

a. **Land Operations.** The inherent precision of GPS allows precise site surveys, emplacement of artillery, target acquisition, and navigation. GPS establishes a "common reference grid" within the operational area, enables a "common time," helps establish "common direction," and facilitates synchronized operations. Some of the benefits of using GPS include:

(1) Mine fields and obstacles can be accurately surveyed, emplaced, and recorded.

(2) The accuracy of artillery fire is improved through precise gun emplacement, precision gun laying, precision observer location, reduced target location error, and precision guided artillery and mortar rounds. Accuracy also considerably enhances the effects of massing artillery fires and facilitates fire support coordination measures.

(3) Armored, mechanized, and wheeled units can travel "buttoned-up" and still maintain highly accurate position awareness.

(4) Exact location and navigation information helps logistic support by expediting resupply efforts. The precise information also supports the timely and efficient evacuation of wounded personnel to aid stations.

(5) Enables FFT.

(6) Enhances air support.

b. **Maritime Operations**

(1) Ships and submarines can precisely plot their position, thereby allowing safe port operations and navigation through restricted waters.

(2) Coastlines can be accurately surveyed by using a combination of laser range finding and highly accurate position information.

(3) Mines can be laid and precisely plotted for friendly force avoidance and safe, efficient retrieval.

(4) Rendezvous at sea, sea rescue, and other operations that require precise tracking can be facilitated using space-based PNT support.

The Global Positioning System Space, Control, and User Segments

Space Segment

Legacy (Block IIA/IIR)	Modernized (Block IIR-M)	Modernized (Block IIF)
• Basic GPS • C/A civil signal (L1C/A) • Standard positioning service • Precise positioning service • L1 & L2 P (Y) Nav • NDS	• 2nd civil signal (L2C) • M-code signals (L1M, L2M) • Flex AJ power (+7 dB)	• 3rd civil signal (L5)

Control Segment

Legacy	Upgraded (AEP)	Modernized (OCX V1)
• TT&C • L1 & L2 monitoring	• IIR-M IIF TT&C • WAGE, AII, LADO • SAASM • New MCS/AMCS	• New architecture • Signal monitoring • M-code

User Segment

Legacy	Upgraded		Modernized
• PLGR	• DAGR • C SEL • ADAP	• GAS-1 • MAGR/2K • GB-GRAM	• MGUE • MUE • MSR

Legend

IIA	block IIA	L2C	civil signal on the L2 frequency
IIF	block II follow on	L2M	M-code on the L2 frequency
IIR	block II replenishment	LADO	launch and early orbit, anomaly resolution and disposal operations
IIR-M	block II replenishment – modernized		
ADAP	advanced digital antenna production	MAGR/2K	miniaturized airborne GPS receiver (2000)
AEP	architectural evolution program	M-code	military code
AII	accuracy improvement initiative	MCS	master control station
AJ	anti-jam	MGUE	military GPS user equipment
AMCS	alternate master control station	MSR	modernized space receiver
C/A	coarse acquisition	MUE	modernized user equipment
C SEL	combat survivor/evader location	Nav	navagation
DAGR	defense advanced GPS receiver	NDS	nuclear detonation detection system
dB	dec bel	OCX	operational control segment
Flex	flexible	P (Y)	precise code
GAS-1	GPS antenna system	PLGR	precision lightweight GPS receiver
GB-GRAM	ground-based GPS received application module	SAASM	selective availability anti-spoofing module
		TT & C	telemetry, tracking, and commanding
GPS	Global Positioning System	WAGE	wide area GPS enhancement
L1M	M-code on the L1 frequency		

Figure E-1. The Global Positioning System Space, Control, and User Segments

(5) PNT enables precision weapons delivery as well as missile warning and defeat.

c. **Air Operations**

(1) Information on PNT enhances airdrop, air refueling, SAR, reconnaissance, terminal approach and recovery, low-level navigation, targeting, and precision weapons delivery.

(2) Air corridors for friendly return-to-force procedures can be set with greater accuracy, and aircraft have a greater capability to safely follow these corridors.

(3) Nontraditional ISR and dynamic targeting enables near-real-time reallocation of airborne firepower.

d. **Space Operations.** The GPS navigation service provides exact positioning to other satellites to enable their "position autonomy." The same service enables "orbital rendezvous" between space systems (e.g., space docking for the Soyuz or other replenishment vehicle with the International Space Station). It also provides precise time to communications satellites and to systems in geosynchronous orbits. New launch vehicles rely upon GPS position and derived velocity information to aid in determining attitude orientation.

e. **Navigation Warfare.** NAVWAR encompasses various offensive, defensive and support operations to ensure unimpeded availability of PNT information for the US and its multinational partners and, when necessary, deny PNT information to an adversary. NAVWAR is a cross-domain (air, land, sea, space, and cyberspace) and cross-mission area capability enabled by taskable space systems, EMS operations, civil-military unity of effort, and alternate sources of PNT information. NAVWAR should be a consideration in all joint planning.

3. **Advantages**

a. **Accuracy.** The GPS constellation provides continuous global service. Accuracy of the service is provided by the type of receiver used, the number of satellites in view, and the geometric configuration of those satellites.

b. **Accessibility.** Because GPS equipment is passive, it is capable of providing continuous real-time information. Any authorized user with a keyed PPS receiver has access to the most precise PNT information. However, commercial user equipment cannot receive and process the PPS information and is limited to the SPS signal.

c. **Graceful Degradation.** Each GPS satellite can store information onboard for up to 60 days. In the event the GPS constellation cannot be updated, accuracy will gradually degrade. The rate of degradation is very slow in the first few days but increases with time. This allows GPS to be used for several days even if the update capabilities are interrupted.

d. **Common Grid.** The default navigation grid used by the GPS is the WGS-84. WGS-84 can be easily converted to any grid reference using the terminal device.

e. **Jamming.** Space-based navigation systems (e.g., GPS) are susceptible to jamming and interference. The use of GPS encryption (like a more robust military code) and nulling antennas/filters, as well as the correct placement of GPS receivers on various platforms, improves jamming resistance. Tactical measures employed by joint forces decrease vulnerability from ground-based jamming (such as placing a hand-held receiver at the bottom of a foxhole). Integration of GPS with other sources of PNT, such as inertial navigation systems, can make a PNT solution even more robust to GPS jamming.

f. **Anti-Spoofing (A/S).** With the precise capability provided by the GPS, a logical concern is that an adversary could generate false signals to mislead an authorized user with respect to position or timing information. A/S technology is designed to mitigate receiver confusion that could be caused by intentionally misleading transmissions.

4. Limitations

a. Adversary exploitation of the SPS can reduce the US military advantage. Commercial GPS receivers are vulnerable to jamming.

b. Jamming GPS can adversely affect civil and first responder operations, as well as joint military operations within a geographic area. The stronger the jammer, the larger the affected area. To account for potential GPS jamming, CCDRs and their subordinate JFCs factor it into their EW plans. Consideration must also be given to friendly interference, which is mitigated via the joint restricted frequency list. Coordination procedures for this list are detailed in JP 3-13.1, *Electronic Warfare*.

c. Signals from at least four satellites are required to build a three-dimensional position and navigation picture (only one signal is needed for timing). Units relying on hand-held GPS receivers in areas of dense vegetation or steep terrain may have diminished GPS capabilities due to the lack of LOS reception of GPS signals.

d. GPS navigation signals are also affected by ionospheric scintillation, tropospheric errors, and signal multipath issues. Receivers capable of two frequency reception minimize errors.

e. Denial of the GPS "navigation" signal may have a direct negative impact on joint systems that have nothing to do with "navigation." This is particularly true for communications systems that rely on GPS timing.

Intentionally Blank

APPENDIX F
OPERATIONALLY RESPONSIVE SPACE

1. Overview

a. Per Deputy Secretary of Defense Memorandum dated 9 July 2007, ORS is defined as "assured space power focused on timely satisfaction of JFCs' needs." ORS provides a means to synchronize and integrate space capabilities in time and purpose with the employment of other forces by the JFC. ORS also provides the "capacity to respond to unexpected loss or degradation of selected capabilities, and/or provide timely availability of tailored or new capabilities" (per National Security Presidential Directive [NSPD]-40, *US Space Transportation Policy*). In doing so, ORS balances the requirement to meet JFC urgent space needs with the need to innovate when adapting space capabilities to changing requirements. Strategic or long-term needs are not a primary focus of ORS.

b. **Establishing Needs.** The CDRUSSTRATCOM validates system requirements for systems to be acquired by the ORS Office and provides operational oversight for all ORS activities consistent with the UCP and other applicable authorities. This includes collecting, prioritizing, and managing identified joint force needs, and coordinating ORS capabilities to meet those needs.

c. **Capability Development.** The ORS Office is a joint organization established under Section 2273a of Title 10, USC. The mission of the office is to develop enabling capabilities to fulfill joint military operational requirements for on-demand space support and reconstitution, and to coordinate and execute ORS efforts across DOD with respect to planning, acquisition, and operations. Collaboration by the ORS Office with DOD, IC, and other national security space mission partners ensures a range of solutions are considered when providing responsive, actionable, and near-real-time space capabilities to commanders and other users. The ORS Office expedites development and fielding of capabilities by architecting and demonstrating operational prototypes to both satisfy short-term urgent needs and illustrate proof of concepts in anticipation of eventual operational fielding through established acquisition processes.

2. Application

a. ORS missions can support USSTRATCOM space mission areas of space force enhancement, space control, and space support by providing timely, responsive space capabilities when needed.

b. To accomplish these missions, ORS capabilities are implemented in a three tiered approach:

(1) Tier-1 uses existing or on-station capabilities to create highly responsive space effects through the employment, modification, and revised application of these space capabilities. The targeted timeframe for the application of Tier-1 solutions is immediately-to-days from the time the need is identified. Tier-1 solutions focus on existing ground and space systems, operations, and procedures. Although mission or system utilization analysis

OPERATIONALLY RESPONSIVE SPACE

A successful example of an operationally responsive space (ORS) space force enhancement capability delivery is ORS-1.

In late 2007, Joint Functional Component Command for Space and United States Central Command (USCENTCOM) requested a solution to overcome an impending shortfall in intelligence, surveillance, and reconnaissance (ISR) capabilities.

This shortfall was the result of normal degradation of on-orbit systems, in concert with schedule slips to the replacement system. In April of 2008, Commander, United States Strategic Command (CDRUSSTRATCOM) validated this need and initiated the ORS process by tasking the ORS Office to assess the need and develop conceptual solutions. The ORS Office formed an interagency team which further defined the requirements, collected input from the broader space community (including industry), and developed a solution set. These solution options were presented to CDRUSSTRATCOM, and the decision was made to request execution of the ORS-1 satellite mission as the selected course of action.

In October of 2008, the ORS Executive Committee, led by the Executive Agent for space, approved ORS-1. Over the ensuing 30 months, the ORS Office developed the complete ORS-1 mission (spacecraft; payload; launch; command and control; tracking, processing, exploitation, and dissemination) with extensive input from USCENTCOM.

On June 28, 2011, the ORS-1 satellite was launched into low-earth orbit by the Minotaur-1 launcher from National Aeronautics and Space Administration's Wallops Flight Facility. One interesting aspect of the ORS-1 capability is the manner in which this system seamlessly integrates into USCENTCOM's existing architecture for tasking ISR collection systems and receiving products in return. The key to this architecture is the adapted use of the Planning Tool for Resource, Integration, Synchronization, and Management (PRISM) system within the USCENTCOM Joint Intelligence Operations Center. PRISM is the mechanism used by USCENTCOM to task many airborne ISR collection platforms, including the high-altitude U2 system. By adopting PRISM as the means for tasking the ORS-1 satellite, the ORS-1 system was easily integrated into the USCENTCOM capability set. In a similar manner, use of the 513th Military Intelligence Brigade to process and exploit the ORS-1 imagery resulted in re-use of an existing processing, exploitation, and dissemination process, for which USCENTCOM had a high level of familiarity.

Various Sources

may be needed, Tier-1 solutions will not typically involve the design, engineering, or fabrication of new materiel items.

(2) If all possible Tier-1 options have been evaluated and no Tier-1 solution can respond to the need, a Tier-2 solution will be considered. Tier-2 solutions will utilize field-

ready capabilities or deploy new or additional capabilities that are field-ready. The targeted timeframe for delivering usable Tier-2 solutions is days-to-weeks from the time the JFC need is established. Tier-2 solutions focus on achieving responsive exploitation, augmentation, or reconstitution of space force enhancement or space control capabilities through rapid assembly, integration, testing, and deployment of affordable small satellites.

(3) There may be cases where an expressed need cannot be addressed through existing capabilities (Tier-1) or through rapid deployment of field-ready capabilities (Tier-2). In such events, ORS efforts must focus on the rapid development and deployment of a new capability (Tier-3). Once developed, Tier-3 capabilities will be responsively deployed and employed in the same manner as Tier-2 assets. The targeted timeframe for the presentation of an operational Tier-3 capability is months-to-1-year of the established JFC need. Meeting this challenging timeline cannot be accomplished unless the amount of new development involved is very limited.

c. To develop capabilities, ORS leverages existing technology and capabilities to maximize their benefits. This includes exploring non-space options as well as other materiel and nonmateriel solutions.

3. Advantages

ORS helps to synchronize and integrate space capabilities in time and purpose with the employment of other forces by a JFC. Advantages of ORS include:

a. Rapid presentation of new or enhanced space capabilities in response to JFC needs. These capabilities will be operational within one year of that need.

b. Rapidly adapt or augment existing space capabilities when needed to expand operational capability.

c. Rapidly reconstitute or replenish critical space capabilities to preserve operational capability, providing the JFC assured, persistent space power.

4. Limitations

a. Shortened timelines will challenge every aspect of the development and deployment process and potentially increase risk.

b. Congressionally suggested cost ceilings will require very well-defined JFC needs. In turn, these will drive minimal developmental approaches. These cost ceilings may affect the ability to place satellites in other than LEO; however, there is nothing to restrict ORS satellites from taking advantage of a ride-share to MEO or geosynchronous Earth orbit (GEO).

*Operationally Responsive Space-1, prior to launch
at Wallops Flight Facility, VA.*

APPENDIX G
SPACE FUNDAMENTALS

1. General

a. Space is a domain enabling many joint force-essential capabilities. These capabilities derive from exploitation of the unique characteristics of space, among which include a global perspective and lack of overflight restrictions, as well as the speed and persistence afforded by satellites.

(1) **Global Perspective.** Space has been labeled "the ultimate high ground" for good reason. Even LEO satellites, which are relatively close to Earth's surface (altitudes from roughly one hundred miles to a few hundred miles), have fields of view spanning hundreds of miles. At greater distances, GEO satellites can view slightly over one-third of the Earth at once. At this range, only three evenly-positioned GEO satellites are needed to provide almost complete global communications coverage (regions near the North and South Poles cannot be covered by GEO satellites due to reasons discussed below). Thus, space affords a global vantage point from which to assess several considerations, from tactical to strategic levels.

(2) **Lack of Overflight Restrictions.** Unlike the international rules for overflight of state aircraft, under which nations may prevent—using force, if needed—aircraft overflight, there are no international satellite overflight restrictions. Thus, space provides unhindered access to points spanning the globe. It is this unhindered capability of ISR, communications, and navigation coupled with the ability to traverse the globe in very short periods that provide capabilities unrivaled by other domains.

(3) **Speed and Persistence.** Satellites travel at incredible rates of speed and, unlike aircraft, do not require constant propulsion to remain in orbit. These factors enable satellites not only to cover vast amounts of ground in very short periods of time, but also to provide continuous operation and coverage. Often, a satellite's life-span is limited only by the reliability of its onboard systems and the quantity of propellant available for station keeping and additional maneuvers.

b. All of these unique aspects make space a very desirable domain within which to operate. However, space also has many peculiar characteristics which must be appreciated by joint forces to plan and operate effectively.

2. Unique Characteristics of Space

While physical laws on land, in the water, or in the air are directly observable and commonly understood at a fundamental level, the physics of Earth-orbiting objects— "satellites"—within the vacuum of space is more difficult to observe and understand. The unique attributes of space have profound implications for the inherent capabilities and limitations that derive from them. Consequently, though a comprehensive discussion of orbital mechanics is neither possible nor desirable within this publication, certain basic precepts must be understood to leverage space power effectively.

a. **Gravitational Forces Predominate.** Due to the Earth's gravitational field, satellites orbiting the Earth are in a constant state of falling toward the Earth's center. At the same time, the satellite is hurtling at extremely high speeds in a direction near-horizontal to the Earth's surface. On average, the Earth's surface curves downward five meters for every eight kilometers traveled horizontally. Consequently, if a satellite is to stay in a simple circular LEO, it must traverse eight kilometers of the Earth's surface in the time required to fall five meters toward the Earth's center. In essence, the Earth's surface will curve away at a rate proportional to the rate the satellite is falling and the satellite will never actually hit the Earth. The horizontal speed required to achieve this circular LEO is roughly 17,500 miles per hour. The speeds required for orbit insertion and the rates at which a satellite falls to Earth are dependent on the altitude and shape of the orbit in question. An orbit is the trajectory or path through space a satellite will follow due to Earth's gravity. The time it takes a satellite to complete one full revolution on its orbit trajectory is known as its period.

b. **Orbits Are Fixed in Space.** With the exception of a few external forces (see "perturbations" discussion below), orbits do not move. That is, a given satellite's orbit is fixed in space, while the Earth rotates beneath the orbit and while the satellite itself races around the orbit like a car on a racetrack. This phenomenon results from the satellite's *angular momentum*. A gyroscope illustrates the effects of angular momentum on a much smaller scale. When holding a spinning gyroscope, it is difficult to twist in various directions. The inertia, or resistance to positional change, is the effect of the gyroscope's angular momentum. Satellites' high altitudes (and thus great radial distances from Earth's center) and very high velocities mean satellites have tremendous angular momenta, implying extremely large inertias and thus orbital planes that are very resistant to movement. Therefore, they are not easily repositioned.

c. **Satellites Are Not Very Maneuverable.** Contrary to popular, but misleading, conceptions about maneuvering in space, satellites cannot maneuver much, if at all, because of the effects of angular momentum. Maneuvering, such as changing an orbit's size or inclination, costs fuel and can severely limit the life of a satellite. As a historical example, if a space shuttle used every bit of onboard fuel to change its orbital plane, the maximum plane change it could effect would amount to no more than two and a half degrees. A more important inference drawn from these limits is that satellites cannot "hover" over a given point on Earth, nor can they "bend" their orbital planes to maneuver to a specified point. Thus, a satellite's arrival over a particular point on the Earth depends almost wholly upon the passage of time, as the Earth rotates through the plane of the satellite's orbit, and the satellite orbits around the Earth.

d. **Orbital Planes Must Pass Through Earth's Center.** Gravity is the predominant force, continuously pulling the satellite toward Earth's center. Because of this phenomenon, any orbit traced by a satellite must be within a plane that passes through the center of the Earth. Practically, this means orbits cannot be designed to be "offset" or "overhead" (e.g., a "halo" orbit over the North Pole) to one side or another from the Earth: each orbit *must* encircle the Earth.

e. **"Perturbations" Can Change an Orbit.** Certain external forces can change the parameters of an orbit, producing an exception to the general rule that orbits are fixed in space. These forces are generally known as "perturbations," because they perturb, or alter, the orbit. These include atmospheric drag (atmospheric particles exist even at very high altitudes, albeit in very low concentrations); gravitational pull of the sun, Moon, and other planets; variations in the Earth's gravitational field, resulting in orbital plane changes and other effects; solar pressure from the sun's radiation; and interactions between solar radiation and the Earth's magnetic field. Perturbations have significant impacts on planning considerations. For example, contrary to popularly held notions about satellite tracking, no country has the ability to continuously track every satellite orbiting Earth. However, if a satellite's position is known at several points, predictive models using basic laws of physics can be used to calculate the satellite's future position. Unfortunately, orbital perturbations can degrade the accuracy of those models. Generally, the lower a satellite's altitude, the shorter the accuracy duration of a given model, and consequently the greater the need for up-to-date prediction data (see paragraph 3, "Operational Considerations").

f. **Certain Orbits Have Special Characteristics.** Certain orbits have features that seemingly violate the general rules discussed above. On closer examination, however, these apparent exceptions are seen nonetheless to follow the general rules.

(1) **Geosynchronous/Geostationary.** Geosynchronous satellites track in their orbit around the Earth at the same rate at which the Earth rotates upon its axis; they are synchronized to the Earth's rotation. Therefore, these satellites have a period of 24 hours. (Note: The Earth makes a rotation around its axis in a sidereal day, about 23 hours and 56 minutes as indicated in Figure G-1; during that time it moves a short distance [about 1 degree] along its orbit around the sun. So after a sidereal day has passed, the Earth still needs to rotate a bit more before the sun reaches its highest point. A solar day is, therefore, nearly 4 minutes longer than a sidereal day.) If placed directly over the equator, to a ground-based observer, a satellite in such an orbit appears to "hover" a little over 22,000 statute miles above that point. However, the satellite is actually moving very fast, in pace with Earth's rotation. This special, but very common, type of geosynchronous orbit is called geostationary because it appears stationary above Earth. GEO orbits allow constant LOS with a given, very large (slightly over one-third of the Earth) footprint, and thus lend themselves readily to gross environmental imagery (i.e., tens-of-square-miles pixel sizes) and global communications. This effect only occurs at this specific altitude and inclination, resulting in a band of valuable space "real estate" known as the Geosynchronous Belt. An exception occurs near the poles, where communication with high north or south latitudes (roughly 75 degrees or greater) is not possible because of a lack of LOS with the satellite.

(2) **Sun-Synchronous.** Natural perturbations will cause satellite orbits to change over time, and mission planners can use this effect to their advantage. Such is the case with sun-synchronous orbits (see Figure G-2). Although often modeled as symmetric, the Earth actually is non-spherical with an asymmetric mass distribution. A cross-section of the Earth is about 44 kilometers wider at the equator than at the poles with varying mass properties (e.g., water versus mountains). This oblateness of the Earth causes an orbital perturbation known as the "J2" effect to alter the orientation and rotation of an orbital plane. By incorporating the J2 effect and carefully selecting the inclination of the orbit, a satellite can be placed in an orbital plane that shifts by slightly less than one degree per day to the east. The result is when the satellite passes over a given point, it will do so with the same sun

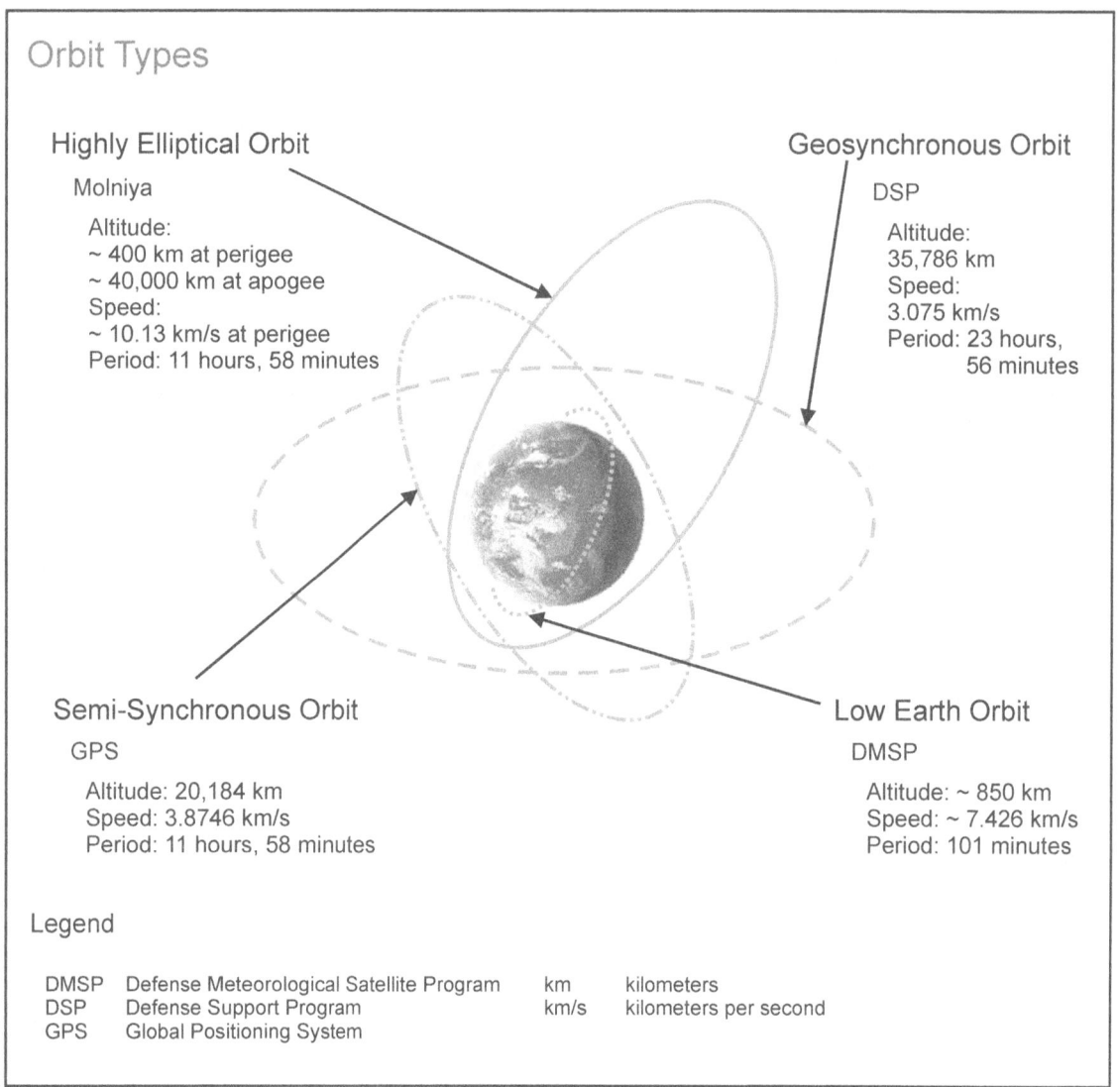

Orbit Types

Highly Elliptical Orbit

Molniya

Altitude:
~ 400 km at perigee
~ 40,000 km at apogee
Speed:
~ 10.13 km/s at perigee
Period: 11 hours, 58 minutes

Geosynchronous Orbit

DSP

Altitude:
35,786 km
Speed:
3.075 km/s
Period: 23 hours,
        56 minutes

Semi-Synchronous Orbit

GPS

Altitude: 20,184 km
Speed: 3.8746 km/s
Period: 11 hours, 58 minutes

Low Earth Orbit

DMSP

Altitude: ~ 850 km
Speed: ~ 7.426 km/s
Period: 101 minutes

Legend

DMSP	Defense Meteorological Satellite Program	km	kilometers
DSP	Defense Support Program	km/s	kilometers per second
GPS	Global Positioning System		

Figure G-1. Orbit Types

angle (hence the label, sun-synchronous). This does not imply that a sun-synchronous satellite passes over the same point every day, only that when the satellite does pass over a given point along its ground track, it will have the same sun angle, and thus, the sun shadows cast by features on the Earth's surface will not change. These types of orbits are particularly useful for reconnaissance and weather applications, where maintaining a constant viewing condition is critical (e.g., height determination, change detection).

(3) **Highly Elliptical Orbit.** An HEO, as its name implies, is a very flat, oval-shaped orbit. The usefulness of such orbits derives from the fact that satellites close to Earth travel quickly, and those further away travel slowly. At their most distant points from Earth, satellites in HEO orbits can be over 25,000 miles away. The relatively slow satellite speeds at these points combined with long orbit tracks provide HEO satellites long dwell times at these distance points, again giving the appearance that satellites in these orbits "hover" for a time being. Such orbits are normally inclined so that these long dwell times occur over high-latitude points on Earth, ideally suiting them for communication satellites serving high-

Sun-Synchronous Orbits

Typical Low Earth Orbit   Sun-Synchronous Orbit

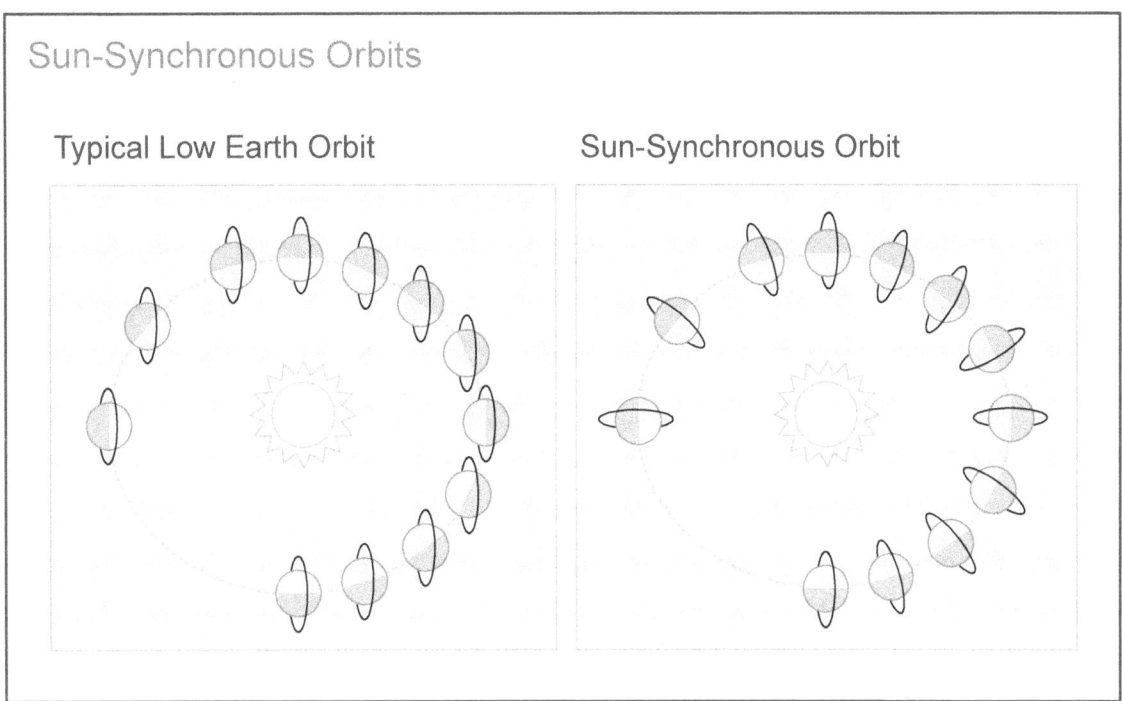

Figure G-2. Sun-Synchronous Orbits

latitude locales (e.g., Russia, Scandinavia, Canada). Although many types of HEO orbits are possible, the most useful is termed a Molniya orbit (from the Russian word for "lightning," so named because of the dramatic speed of the satellite as it passes close to Earth). In general, the oblateness of the Earth perturbs the argument of perigee, so that even if the apogee started near the North Pole, it would gradually move unless constantly corrected with "station keeping" thruster burns. To avoid this expenditure of fuel, the Molniya orbit uses an inclination of 63.4 degrees, for which these perturbations are zero. This type of orbit, inclined at 63.4 degrees, maintains perigee in the Southern hemisphere so that it dwells in the Northern hemisphere for nearly 11 hours of its 12-hour period. Three satellites set in phased Molniya orbits could thus provide continuous Northern-tier coverage. Other applications include weather and ISR. A variety of commonly used orbit types and their parameters are described in Figure G-1.

(4) **Lagrangian Orbits.** While the above orbits are used for the vast majority of DOD satellites, there are other useful orbits including Lagrangian orbits. Five points (L1-L5) near any two large objects in space (e.g., the Earth and Moon) are within both bodies' influence and revolve around the larger body at the same rate as smaller body. These points are ideal locations for sun-observing satellites such as the Solar Heliospheric Observatory—a joint European Space Agency-NASA mission) (Ka) was launched in December 1995 and NASA's Advanced Composition Explorer satellite was launched in August 1997. Both of these satellites orbit the sun near the L1 Lagrange point between Earth and the sun—a unique orbit where the satellite stays on the line between the sun and Earth, where their gravities balance. In this orbit, these satellites have a prime view of the solar wind and provide near-real-time, 24/7 continuous coverage of solar wind parameters and solar energetic particle intensities (for example, coronal mass ejections and solar flares which can

disrupt radio transmissions and cause damage to satellites and electrical transmission line facilities, resulting in potentially massive and long lasting power outages).

(5) **Low Earth Orbit.** There is no formal definition of LEO but it is generally considered to have an apogee of no more than 1000 kilometers from farthest point from the point in the orbit to the center of the earth. At low altitudes, atmospheric drag will limit a satellite's life unless it is boosted periodically into a higher altitude, therefore operational life will be dependent on the amount of fuel available. At an altitude of 320 kilometers, without any boosting, operational life would be expected to be around one year, increasing to around 10 years at an altitude of 800 kilometers. LEO is ideal for observation, environmental monitoring, small communications satellites, and science instrument payloads. Manned orbital objects, such as the International Space Station, generally remain below 500 kilometers to prevent the need for heavy shielding to protect the crew from Van Allen belt radiation. Objects in LEO have the advantage that they pass relatively close to the Earth, so they can use less powerful sensors and transmitters, but will only be in the view of a ground user or station for the short period of time when overhead. For this reason, for some applications it is usual to provide a constellation of several satellites spaced around the same or similar orbits to provide continuous coverage. A satellite in circular LEO with an altitude of 850 kilometers will travel at a speed of 24,600 kilometers per hour, about 7 kilometers per second, and have a period of 101 minutes.

(6) **Medium Earth Orbit.** Additionally, there is no formal definition of MEO, but by convention it is considered to include those orbits between LEO and geostationary orbit. A semi-synchronous orbit is a special case of a MEO which has a nearly circular orbit which repeats an identical ground trace twice each day; hence the term semi-synchronous. The GPS satellites use this type of orbit, at an altitude of around 20,830 kilometers and speed of around 14,330 kilometers per hour.

g. **One Satellite Often Is Not Enough.** No "one-size-fits-all" satellite exists for every application. Even satellites perfectly optimized for a particular mission may lack the required coverage for that mission. In such cases, a *constellation*—multiple satellites performing a single mission—is used to provide increased coverage or timeliness to meet mission requirements. For example, navigation constellations (such as GPS) are designed to ensure that signals from at least four satellites can be simultaneously received at any location on the ground, enabling three-dimensional position fixing unavailable using only a single GPS satellite. Other examples include communications constellations, which are designed to ensure continuous connectivity between both ends of the communications link. To provide truly global coverage, such systems may include both equatorial and polar components. A final example includes weather and reconnaissance systems, which typically require constellations that combine both high and low altitude components. This construct provides a capability to combine wide-area, low-resolution coverage with limited field-of-view, high-resolution coverage to provide a complete weather picture. Regardless of configuration, constellations are designed to optimize mission components across multiple satellites so that overall mission requirements are met.

3. Operational Considerations

The unique characteristics of space drive important operational considerations that must be weighed when planning to provide space services and capabilities to the joint force:

a. **Revisit Rates.** "Revisit rate" refers to the interval between successive passes of a satellite over the same point on the Earth. Revisit rates are dependent on the geometry of the orbit itself, as well as its period (the time required for a satellite to complete one orbit). The larger the orbit, the longer the period will be. For example, typical LEO periods average from 90 minutes to a few hours. During this time, the Earth will continue to rotate on its axis beneath the orbit. Thus, by the time the satellite completes one orbit, its track over the Earth has shifted appreciably. Revisit rates for some satellites are as much as several days, while other satellites have much shorter revisit rates, depending on the orbit. In the extreme, GEO satellites have no revisit rate, since these satellites constantly maintain LOS with particular sectors of the Earth.

b. **Access Windows.** "Access window" refers to the amount of time a given satellite will be able to maintain LOS geometry with a fixed point on Earth's surface. With the exception of satellites in GEO and HEO orbits, a satellite cannot dwell over a fixed point for any prolonged length of time. The closer a satellite is to the Earth's surface, the faster it will travel, and the smaller the field of view available to that satellite. LEO satellites, for example, can maintain sensor contact and/or communications with a fixed point for only about 10 to 15 minutes. Access times and fields of view for other satellites increase proportionally to increasing satellite altitudes. Just as knowledge of friendly access windows ensures timely satellite contact, knowledge of enemy access windows helps in planning appropriate countertactics.

c. **Currency of Predictive Data.** Parameters describing a given satellite's position in space are derived from various sensors' observations of the satellite's azimuth, elevation, and range. These position "snapshots" are used to predict future satellite locations. Generally, the lower a satellite's orbital altitude, the shorter the time window within which a given prediction will remain accurate, because aggregate perturbation impacts (such as atmospheric drag) increase in severity with decreasing altitude. Consequently, for satellites in LEO, predictive models usually cannot provide accuracy within required tolerances beyond roughly one or two days. For the field-deployed joint force, this fact drives the need to ensure data sets are as current as possible for all orbits, increasing in importance for orbits closest to Earth.

d. **Electromagnetic Interference.** Every capability leveraged from space derives from the EMS, whether the capability enables ISR, communications, or navigation. All of these capabilities are thus subject to disturbances known as EMI. EMI can be natural or man-made. An example of natural EMI derives from effects caused by Earth's ionosphere. This outer region of Earth's atmosphere consists of ionized atmospheric gases that create random noise within the EMS. However, this is not a uniform region. The sun's electromagnetic energy and the Earth's magnetic field interact in complex ways to strengthen or weaken this interference, with both global and local impacts. Understanding and predicting these impacts help to mitigate their effect through preparation (e.g., selecting different operating frequencies, boosting power, timing transmissions to occur during periods of minimum interference). This understanding also helps in space control, where employment of capabilities can be masked by, and/or attributed to, environmental impacts. An example of man-made EMI is drawn from jamming, where a stronger electromagnetic signal is used to overpower a weaker signal. Knowledge of the space domain and of threat capabilities can help mitigate both natural and man-made EMI.

e. **Lack of Serviceability.** Normally, space assets are not serviceable after launch (the Hubble Space Telescope, International Space Station, being the most common exceptions). This means that their ability to change functions, recover from failures or attacks, or maneuver is based almost entirely on the design of the system at the time of deployment (some software uploads may be possible). This limits flexibility compared to terrestrial assets which can be serviced, repaired, or upgraded. Lack of serviceability puts tighter constraints on the operational C2 since some requests can reduce the asset lifetime (e.g., too much fuel expenditure or too much battery depletion during eclipses).

APPENDIX H
REFERENCES

The development of JP 3-14 is based upon the following primary references:

1. **Federal Law**

    a. Title 10, USC.

    b. Goldwater-Nichols Department of Defense Reorganization Act of 1986.

2. **Strategy and Policy Documents**

    a. *The National Security Strategy of the United States.*

    b. *The National Defense Strategy of the United States.*

    c. *National Military Strategy.*

    d. NSPD-27, *US Commercial Remote Sensing Space Policy.*

    e. NSPD-39, *US Space-Based Positioning, Navigation, and Timing Policy.*

    f. NSPD-40, *US Space Transportation Policy.*

    g. *National Space Policy of the United States of America.*

    h. Unified Command Plan.

    i. *National Security Space Strategy.*

    j. Presidential Policy Directive-4, *National Space Policy.*

3. **Office of the Secretary of Defense Guidance**

    a. DODD 3100.16, *DOD Management of Space Professional Development.*

    b. Report to Congressional Defense Committees, *DOD Plan for Operationally Responsive Space.*

    c. DOD Global Positioning System Security Policy.

4. **Department of Defense**

    a. DODD 3100.10, *Department of Defense Space Policy.*

    b. DODD 4650.05, *Positioning, Navigation, and Timing (PNT).*

    c. DODD 5100.01, *Functions of the Department of Defense and Its Major Components.*

d. DODD 5105.19, *Defense Information Systems Agency (DISA)*.

e. DODD 5105.60, *National Geospatial-Intelligence Agency (NGA)*.

f. DODD 5105.62, *Defense Threat Reduction Agency*.

g. DODI 3100.12, *Space Support*.

h. DODI S-3100.13, *Space Force Application*.

i. DODI S-3100.14, *Space Force Enhancement*.

j. DODI S-3100.15, *Space Control*.

5. **Chairman of the Joint Chiefs of Staff**

a. CJCSI 3110.01H, *2010 Joint Strategic Capabilities Plan (JSCP)*.

b. CJCSI 3910.01A, *Friendly Force Tracking Operations Guidance*.

c. CJCSI 6130.01D, *2007 CJCS Master Positioning, Navigation, and Timing Plan (MPNTP)*.

d. CJCSI 6210.02B, *Information and Operational Architecture of the Integrated Tactical Warning and Attack Assessment System*.

e. CJCSI 6250.01D, *Satellite Communications*.

f. CJCSM 3122.01A, *Joint Operation Planning and Execution System (JOPES) Volume I, Planning Policies and Procedures*.

g. CJCSM 3122.03C, *Joint Operation Planning and Execution System (JOPES) Volume II, Planning Formats*.

h. CJCSM 3219.01C, *Interruption of Remote Sensing Space System Data Collection and Distribution During Periods of National Security Crisis*.

6. **Joint Publications**

a. JP 1, *Doctrine for the Armed Forces of the United States*.

b. JP 1-02, *Department of Defense Dictionary of Military and Associated Terms*.

c. JP 2-01, *Joint and National Intelligence Support to Military Operations*.

d. JP 2-01.3, *Joint Intelligence Preparation of the Operational Environment*.

e. JP 2-03, *Geospatial Intelligence Support to Joint Operations*.

f. JP 3-0, *Joint Operations*.

g. JP 3-01, *Countering Air and Missile Threats*.

h. JP 3-05, *Special Operations*.

i. JP 3-08, *Interorganizational Coordination During Joint Operations*.

j. JP 3-12, *Cyberspace Operations*.

k. JP 3-13, *Information Operations*.

l. JP 3-13.1, *Electronic Warfare*.

m. JP 3-16, *Multinational Operations*.

n. JP 3-27, *Homeland Defense*.

o. JP 3-30, *Command and Control for Joint Air Operations*.

p. JP 3-59, *Meteorological and Oceanographic Operations*.

q. JP 3-60, *Joint Targeting*.

r. JP 4-0, *Joint Logistics*.

s. JP 5-0, *Joint Operation Planning*.

t. JP 6-0, *Joint Communications System*.

7. International Law

a. Treaty on Principles Governing the Activities of States in the Exploration and Use of Outer Space, Including the Moon and Other Celestial Bodies, 1967.

b. Convention on the Prohibition of Military or Any Other Hostile Use of Environmental Modification Techniques, 1977.

c. Charter of the United Nations, 1945.

8. Service Publications

a. Air Force Doctrine Document 3-14, *Space Operations*.

b. Army Regulation 115-11, *Geospatial Information and Services*.

c. Army Regulation 900-1, *Army Space Policy*.

d. Field Manual 3-14, *Space in Support of Army Operations.*

e. Chief of Naval Operations Instruction 5400.43, *Navy Space Policy Implementation.*

9. Supporting Documents

a. CDRUSSTRATCOM CONPLAN 8035 (Change 2).

b. CDRUSSTRATCOM Operational Directive for JFCC SPACE.

c. CDRUSSTRATCOM, Strategic Command Instruction 534-5, *Space-Based Joint Blue Force Situational Awareness (SB-JBFSA) Support to Combatant Commands and Allies.*

d. CDRUSSTRATCOM Concept of Operations, *Operationally Responsive Space (ORS).*

e. CDRUSSTRATCOM, Strategic Instruction 534-19, *Operationally Responsive Space.*

f. JFCC SPACE Concept of Operations.

g. Industrial College of the Armed Forces/National Defense University, Space Industry Study.

h. SI 714-02, *SATCOM System Expert (SSE) and Consolidated SSE (C-SSE) Responsibilities.*

i. SI 714-03, *Satellite Communications (SATCOM) Support Center (SSC) Management.*

j. SI 714-05, *Satellite Communications (SATCOM) Electromagnetic Interference (EMI) Resolution Procedures.*

k. SI 714-05, *Space System Electromagnetic Interference (EMI) Resolution Procedures.*

APPENDIX J
ADMINISTRATIVE INSTRUCTIONS

1. User Comments

Users in the field are highly encouraged to submit comments on this publication to: Joint Staff J-7, Deputy Director, Joint and Coalition Warfighting, Joint and Coalition Warfighting Center, ATTN: Joint Doctrine Support Division, 116 Lake View Parkway, Suffolk, VA 23435-2697. These comments should address content (accuracy, usefulness, consistency, and organization), writing, and appearance.

2. Authorship

The lead agent for this publication is the US Strategic Command. The Joint Staff doctrine sponsor for this publication is the Director for Operations (J-3).

3. Supersession

This publication supersedes JP 3-14, 06 January 2009, *Space Operations*.

4. Change Recommendations

a. Recommendations for urgent changes to this publication should be submitted:

TO: JOINT STAFF WASHINGTON DC//J7-JEDD//

b. Routine changes should be submitted electronically to the Deputy Director, Joint and Coalition Warfighting, Joint and Coalition Warfighting Center, Joint Doctrine Support Division and info the lead agent and the Director for Joint Force Development, J-7/JEDD.

c. When a Joint Staff directorate submits a proposal to the CJCS that would change source document information reflected in this publication, that directorate will include a proposed change to this publication as an enclosure to its proposal. The Services and other organizations are requested to notify the Joint Staff J-7 when changes to source documents reflected in this publication are initiated.

5. Distribution of Publications

Local reproduction is authorized and access to unclassified publications is unrestricted. However, access to and reproduction authorization for classified JPs must be in accordance with DOD Manual 5200.01, Volume 1, *DOD Information Security Program: Overview, Classification, and Declassification,* and DOD Manual 5200.01, Volume 3, *DOD Information Security Program: Protection of Classified Information.*

6. Distribution of Electronic Publications

a. Joint Staff J-7 will not print copies of JPs for distribution. Electronic versions are available on JDEIS at https://jdeis.js.mil (NIPRNET) and http://jdeis.js.smil.mil (SIPRNET), and on the JEL at http://www.dtic.mil/doctrine (NIPRNET).

b. Only approved JPs and joint test publications are releasable outside the CCMDs, Services, and Joint Staff. Release of any classified JP to foreign governments or foreign nationals must be requested through the local embassy (Defense Attaché Office) to DIA, Defense Foreign Liaison/IE-3, 200 MacDill Blvd., Joint Base Anacostia-Bolling, Washington, DC 20340-5100.

c. JEL CD-ROM. Upon request of a joint doctrine development community member, the Joint Staff J-7 will produce and deliver one CD-ROM with current JPs. This JEL CD-ROM will be updated not less than semi-annually and when received can be locally reproduced for use within the CCMDs and Services.

GLOSSARY
PART I—ABBREVIATIONS AND ACRONYMS

AEHF	advanced extremely high frequency
AF	Air Force
AFSCN	Air Force Satellite Control Network
AFSPC	Air Force Space Command
AFSTRAT	Air Forces Strategic
AFWA	Air Force Weather Agency
AJ	anti-jam
AOI	area of interest
AOR	area of responsibility
A/S	anti-spoofing
BDA	battle damage assessment
BMDS	ballistic missile defense system
C2	command and control
CBRN	chemical, biological, radiological, and nuclear
CCDR	combatant commander
CCMD	combatant command
CDRUSSTRATCOM	Commander, United States Strategic Command
CHCSS	Chief, Central Security Service
CJCS	Chairman of the Joint Chiefs of Staff
CJCSI	Chairman of the Joint Chiefs of Staff instruction
CJCSM	Chairman of the Joint Chiefs of Staff manual
C-NAF	component numbered air force
CO	cyberspace operations
COA	course of action
COCOM	combatant command (command authority)
COG	center of gravity
COMAFFOR	commander, Air Force forces
COMFLTCYBERCOM	Commander, Fleet Cyber Command
COMSEC	communications security
COMTENTHFLT	Commander, Tenth Fleet
CONOPS	concept of operations
CONPLAN	concept plan
COP	common operational picture
CSA	combat support agency
C-SMPP	Consolidated Satellite Communications Management Policies and Procedures
CSS	central security service
C-SSE	consolidated satellite communications system expert
DEFSMAC	Defense Special Missile and Aerospace Center
DI&E	data integration and exploitation

DIA	Defense Intelligence Agency
DIRNSA	Director, National Security Agency
DIRSPACEFOR	director of space forces (USAF)
DISA	Defense Information Systems Agency
DMSP	Defense Meteorological Satellite Program
DNI	Director of National Intelligence
DOC	Department of Commerce
DOD	Department of Defense
DODD	Department of Defense directive
DODI	Department of Defense instruction
DODIN	Department of Defense information networks
DSC	defensive space control
DSCA	defense support of civil authorities
D/T/ID	detect/track/identify
DTRA	Defense Threat Reduction Agency
EHF	extremely high frequency
EMI	electromagnetic interference
EMS	electromagnetic spectrum
EW	electronic warfare
FDO	flexible deterrent option
FFT	friendly force tracking
FLTSAT	fleet satellite
FMO	functional manager office
FNMOC	Fleet Numerical Meteorology and Oceanography Center
GAR	gateway access request
GBS	Global Broadcast Service
GCC	geographic combatant commander
GEO	geosynchronous Earth orbit
GEOINT	geospatial intelligence
GI&S	geospatial information and services
GPS	Global Positioning System
HEO	highly elliptical orbit
HN	host nation
HQ	headquarters
IA	information assurance
IC	intelligence community
IGO	intergovernmental organization
IO	information operations
ISR	intelligence, surveillance, and reconnaissance

J-2	intelligence directorate of a joint staff
JFC	joint force commander
JFCC-GS	Joint Functional Component Command for Global Strike
JFCC-IMD	Joint Functional Component Command for Integrated Missile Defense
JFCC-ISR	Joint Functional Component Command for Intelligence, Surveillance, and Reconnaissance (USSTRATCOM)
JFCC-Space	Joint Functional Component Command for Space (USSTRATCOM)
JIPOE	joint intelligence preparation of the operational environment
JP	joint publication
JSPA	joint satellite communications panel administrator
JSPOC	Joint Space Operations Center
LEO	low Earth orbit
LOO	line of operation
LOS	line of sight
LPD	low probability of detection
LPI	low probability of intercept
MARFORSTRAT	United States Marine Corps Forces, United States Strategic Command
MASINT	measurement and signature intelligence
MDA	Missile Defense Agency
MEO	medium Earth orbit
METOC	meteorological and oceanographic
MILSATCOM	military satellite communications
MNF	multinational force
MOC	maritime operations center
MPNTP	Master Positioning Navigation and Timing Plan
MSIC	Missile and Space Intelligence Center
MUOS	Mobile Users Object System
NASA	National Aeronautics and Space Administration
NASIC	National Air and Space Intelligence Center
NATO	North Atlantic Treaty Organization
NAVOCEANO	Naval Oceanographic Office
NAVWAR	navigation warfare
NGA	National Geospatial-Intelligence Agency
NGIC	National Ground Intelligence Center
NGO	nongovernmental organization
NIPRNET	Nonsecure Internet Protocol Router Network
NOAA	National Oceanic and Atmospheric Administration
NRO	National Reconnaissance Office
NSA	National Security Agency
NSG	National System for Geospatial Intelligence

NSPD	national security Presidential directive
NTIA	National Telecommunications and Information Administration
OE	operational environment
OPCON	operational control
OPIR	overhead persistent infrared
OPLAN	operation plan
ORS	operationally responsive space
OSC	offensive space control
OSEI	operational significant event imagery
PED	processing, exploitation, and dissemination
PI	purposeful interference
PIRT	purposeful interference response team
PNT	positioning, navigation, and timing
POC	point of contact
POES	polar operational environment satellite
PPS	precise positioning service
RF	radio frequency
RPO	rendezvous and proximity operations
RSSC	regional satellite communications support center
SAR	search and rescue
SARSAT	search and rescue satellite-aided tracking
SATCOM	satellite communications
SCA	space coordinating authority
SDB	Satellite Communications Database
SecDef	Secretary of Defense
SEW	shared early warning
SHF	super-high frequency
SI	United States Strategic Command strategic instruction
SIGINT	signals intelligence
SIPRNET	SECRET Internet Protocol Router Network
SPS	standard positioning service
SSA	space situational awareness
SSE	space support element
SSWG	space support working group
SWPC	Space Weather Prediction Center
TACON	tactical control
TES	theater event system
TT&C	telemetry, tracking, and commanding
TW&A	threat warning and assessment

UCP	Unified Command Plan
UFO	ultrahigh frequency follow-on
UHF	ultrahigh frequency
UN	United Nations
USASMDC/ARSTRAT	United States Army Space and Missile Defense Command/Army Forces Strategic Command
USC	United States Code
USCYBERCOM	United States Cyber Command
USG	United States Government
USMC	United States Marine Corps
USNO	United States Naval Observatory
USSTRATCOM	United States Strategic Command
UTC	Coordinated Universal Time
WGS	Wideband Global Satellite Communications
WGS 84	World Geodetic System 1984
WMD	weapons of mass destruction

PART II—TERMS AND DEFINITIONS

Army space support team. None. (Approved for removal from JP 1-02.)

attack assessment. An evaluation of information to determine the potential or actual nature and objectives of an attack for the purpose of providing information for timely decisions. (JP 1-02. SOURCE: JP 3-14)

ballistic missile early warning system. None. (Approved for removal from JP 1-02.)

constellation. A system consisting of a number of like satellites acting in concert to perform a specific mission. (Approved for incorporation into JP 1-02.)

Coordinated Universal Time. None. (Approved for removal from JP 1-02.)

Defense Meteorological Satellite Program. None. (Approved for removal from JP 1-02.)

Defense Satellite Communications System. Geosynchronous military communications satellites that provide high data rate communications for military forces, diplomatic corps, and the White House. Also called **DSCS.** (Approved for incorporation into JP 1-02.)

Defense Support Program. Satellites that provide early warning of missile launches. Also called **DSP.** (Approved for incorporation into JP 1-02.)

defensive space control. Operations conducted to preserve the ability to exploit space capabilities via active and passive actions, while protecting friendly space capabilities from attack, interference, or unintentional hazards. (JP 1-02. SOURCE: JP 3-14)

friendly force tracking. A system that provides commanders and forces with location information about friendly and hostile military forces. (Approved for replacement of "blue force tracking" and its definition in JP 1-02.)

Global Positioning System. A satellite-based radio navigation system operated by the Department of Defense to provide all military, civil, and commercial users with precise positioning, navigation, and timing. Also called **GPS.** (JP 1-02. SOURCE: JP 3-14)

ionosphere. None. (Approved for removal from JP 1-02.)

link encryption. None. (Approved for removal from JP 1-02.)

maneuverable reentry vehicle. None. (Approved for removal from JP 1-02.)

multiple independently targetable reentry vehicle. None. (Approved for removal from JP 1-02.)

multiple reentry vehicle. None. (Approved for removal from JP 1-02.)

multispectral imagery. The image of an object obtained simultaneously in a number of discrete spectral bands. Also called **MSI.** (JP 1-02. SOURCE JP 3-14)

navigation warfare. Deliberate defensive and offensive action to assure and prevent positioning, navigation, and timing information through coordinated employment of space, cyberspace, and electronic warfare operations. Also called **NAVWAR.** (Approved for inclusion in JP 1-02.)

negation. In space operations, active and offensive measures to deceive, disrupt, degrade, deny or destroy space capabilities being used to interfere with or attack United States/allied systems. (Approved for incorporation into JP 1-02.)

offensive space control. Those operations to prevent an adversary's hostile use of United States/third-party space capabilities and services or negate (deceive, disrupt, degrade, deny, or destroy) an adversary's efforts to interfere with or attack United States/allied space systems. Also called **OSC.** (Approved for incorporation into JP 1-02.)

overhead persistent infrared. Those systems originally developed to detect and track foreign intercontinental ballistic missile systems. Also called **OPIR.** (Approved for inclusion in JP 1-02.)

period. The time it takes for a satellite to complete one orbit around the earth. (JP 1-02. SOURCE: JP 3-14)

polar orbit. A satellite orbit that passes over the North and South Poles on each orbit, has an angle of inclination relative to the equator of 90 degrees, and eventually passes over all points on the earth. (Approved for incorporation into JP 1-02.)

prevention. In space usage, measures to preclude an adversary's hostile use of United States or third-party space systems and services. (Approved for incorporation into JP 1-02.)

protection. 1. Preservation of the effectiveness and survivability of mission-related military and nonmilitary personnel, equipment, facilities, information, and infrastructure deployed or located within or outside the boundaries of a given operational area. (JP 3-0) 2. In space usage, active and passive defensive measures to ensure that United States and friendly space systems perform as designed by seeking to overcome an adversary's attempts to negate them and to minimize damage if negation is attempted. (JP 1-02. SOURCE: JP 3-14)

proximity operations. None. (Approved for removal from JP 1-02.)

purposeful interference. None. (Approved for removal from JP 1-02.)

regional satellite communications support center. United States Strategic Command operational element responsible for providing the operational communications planners with a point of contact for accessing and managing satellite communications resources. Also called **RSSC.** (Approved for incorporation into JP 1-02.)

space. None. (Approved for incorporation from JP 1-02.)

space asset. Equipment that is an individual part of a space system, which is or can be placed in space or directly supports space activity terrestrially. (Approved for incorporation into JP 1-02.)

space-based infrared system. None. (Approved for removal from JP 1-02.)

space capability. 1. The ability of a space asset to accomplish a mission. 2. The ability of a terrestrial-based asset to accomplish a mission in or through space. (Approved for incorporation into JP 1-02.)

space control. Operations to ensure freedom of action in space for the United States and its allies and, when directed, deny an adversary freedom of action in space. (Approved for incorporation into JP 1-02.)

space coordinating authority. A commander or individual assigned responsibility for planning, integrating, and coordinating space operations support in the operational area. Also called **SCA.** (Approved for incorporation into JP 1-02.)

space force application. Combat operations in, through, and from space to influence the course and outcome of conflict by holding terrestrial targets at risk. (Approved for incorporation into JP 1-02.)

space force enhancement. Combat support operations and force-multiplying capabilities delivered from space systems to improve the effectiveness of military forces as well as support other intelligence, civil, and commercial users. (Approved for incorporation into JP 1-02.)

space forces. The space and terrestrial systems, equipment, facilities, organizations, and personnel necessary to access, use and, if directed, control space for national security. (JP 1-02. SOURCE: JP 3-14)

space power. The total strength of a nation's capabilities to conduct and influence activities to, in, through, and from space to achieve its objectives. (JP 1-02. SOURCE: JP 3-14)

space sensor. None. (Approved for removal from JP 1-02.)

space situational awareness. Cognizance of the requisite current and predictive knowledge of the space environment and the operational environment upon which space operations depend. (Approved for incorporation into JP 1-02.)

space superiority. The degree of dominance in space of one force over any others that permits the conduct of its operations at a given time and place without prohibitive interference from space-based threats. (Approved for incorporation into JP 1-02.)

space support. Launching and deploying space vehicles, maintaining and sustaining spacecraft on-orbit, rendezvous and proximity operations, disposing of (including deorbiting and recovering) space capabilities, and reconstitution of space forces, if required. (Approved for incorporation into JP 1-02.)

space surveillance. The observation of space and of the activities occurring in space. (Approved for incorporation into JP 1-02.)

space systems. All of the devices and organizations forming the space network. (Approved for incorporation into JP 1-02.)

sun-synchronous orbit. An orbit in which the satellite's orbital plane is at a fixed orientation to the sun, i.e., the orbit precesses about the earth at the same rate that the earth orbits the sun. (Approved for incorporation into JP 1-02.)

terrestrial environment. The Earth's land area, including its man-made and natural surface and sub-surface features, and its interfaces and interactions with the atmosphere and the oceans. (JP 1-02. SOURCE: JP 3-14)

theater event system. Architecture for reporting ballistic missile events, composed of three independent processing and reporting elements: the joint tactical ground stations, tactical detection and reporting, and the space-based infrared system mission control station. Also called **TES.** (Approved for incorporation into JP 1-02.)

very small aperture terminal. None. (Approved for removal from JP 1-02.)

Intentionally Blank

JOINT DOCTRINE PUBLICATIONS HIERARCHY

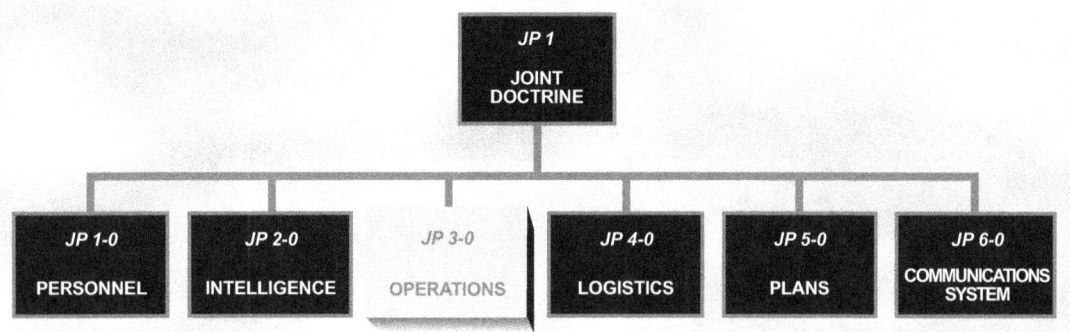

JP 1-0 PERSONNEL	**JP 2-0** INTELLIGENCE	*JP 3-0* OPERATIONS	**JP 4-0** LOGISTICS	**JP 5-0** PLANS	**JP 6-0** COMMUNICATIONS SYSTEM

All joint publications are organized into a comprehensive hierarchy as shown in the chart above. **Joint Publication (JP) 3-14** is in the **Operations** series of joint doctrine publications. The diagram below illustrates an overview of the development process:

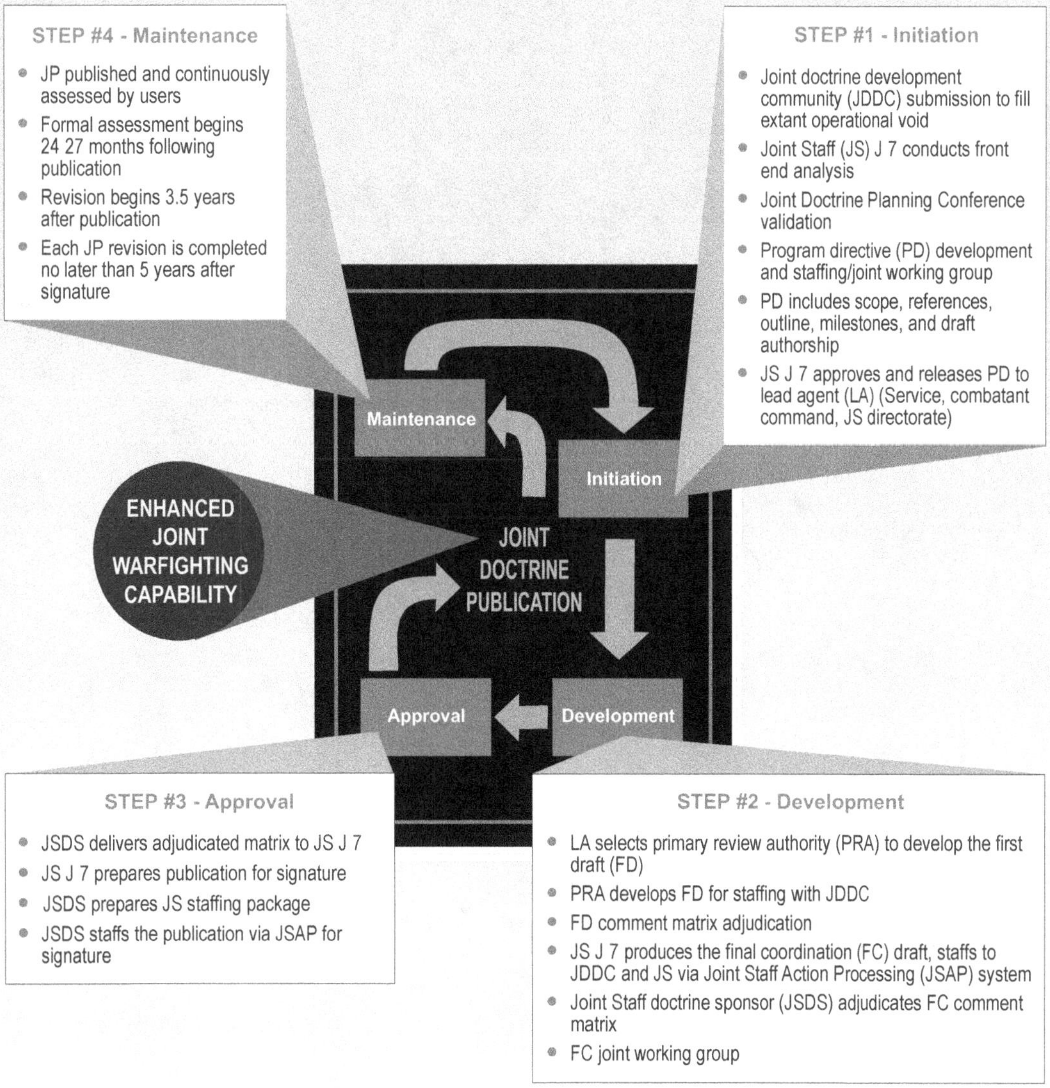

STEP #4 - Maintenance

- JP published and continuously assessed by users
- Formal assessment begins 24 27 months following publication
- Revision begins 3.5 years after publication
- Each JP revision is completed no later than 5 years after signature

STEP #1 - Initiation

- Joint doctrine development community (JDDC) submission to fill extant operational void
- Joint Staff (JS) J 7 conducts front end analysis
- Joint Doctrine Planning Conference validation
- Program directive (PD) development and staffing/joint working group
- PD includes scope, references, outline, milestones, and draft authorship
- JS J 7 approves and releases PD to lead agent (LA) (Service, combatant command, JS directorate)

ENHANCED JOINT WARFIGHTING CAPABILITY

Maintenance

Initiation

JOINT DOCTRINE PUBLICATION

Approval

Development

STEP #3 - Approval

- JSDS delivers adjudicated matrix to JS J 7
- JS J 7 prepares publication for signature
- JSDS prepares JS staffing package
- JSDS staffs the publication via JSAP for signature

STEP #2 - Development

- LA selects primary review authority (PRA) to develop the first draft (FD)
- PRA develops FD for staffing with JDDC
- FD comment matrix adjudication
- JS J 7 produces the final coordination (FC) draft, staffs to JDDC and JS via Joint Staff Action Processing (JSAP) system
- Joint Staff doctrine sponsor (JSDS) adjudicates FC comment matrix
- FC joint working group